I BREAK MY WORD

I BREAK
MY WORD

by

IVOR BROWN

JONATHAN CAPE
THIRTY BEDFORD SQUARE
LONDON

FIRST PUBLISHED NOVEMBER 1951
SECOND IMPRESSION 1953

PRINTED IN GREAT BRITAIN IN THE CITY OF OXFORD
AT THE ALDEN PRESS
BOUND BY A. W. BAIN & CO. LTD., LONDON

FOREWORD

'I NDEED the last word.' So I wrote in the preface of my sixth Word Anthology, *Having the Last Word*, guaranteeing the end of a long-drawn series. And here I am, breaking my word. I had folded up my papers and slammed the desk. And then more papers and letters arrived in flattering plenty. Would I continue? Would I consider these suggestions? Meekly, obediently, untrue to my promise, I have complied. If I make no more pledges, doubtless it will be easier to keep in future the one I have already betrayed.

Once again, I mention with gratitude the correspondents who have been so helpful. If, because of my carelessness or because of their refusal to sign their names legibly — that common and deplorable habit — I have omitted any of my counsellors, I apologize for my own neglect and regret my inability to cope with the script of others. Of course, I owe a perpetual debt to dictionaries of all kinds. It is customary to regard these volumes simply as Works of Reference, dull monsters which you haul from the dusty shelf for occasional consultation. But to me dictionaries are almost continually readable; they are mirrors of the passions and humours of man; they are music in the ear; they are chronicles and maps, history and geography in one. For they show how our names for things have blown about the world on the winds of human policy or of mere chance. Like drifting seeds words settle and flower: they are cultivated, perhaps, in due course by the recipients and given variety of tint and bouquet, as men diversify the rose. The record of these wanderings and changes is as fascinating as any recounting of the human adventure in civilization.

The handicap of the dictionary is that it has to be so big. It is, inevitably, unhandy as a bed-book, that is if it is going to print examples of usage as well as briefly stating the meanings that a word has acquired. The examples are a major pleasure of the reading. That was one reason why I began this series. If there could be such wide delight in anthologies of verse, why not some enjoyment of a kindred basket of picked words? Surely the poet's raw material is worthy of salutation. Anthologies of prose and poetry are numerous, popular and serviceable. The fact of similar choices in many volumes may tend to 'plug' one or two particular and popular pieces by an author who has written much else that is excellent and so to divert attention and curiosity from his larger range of work. That is certainly a pity, but it is also true that many who would not have read him at all may read more of him after meeting him in selection; in any case they do read, instead of over-looking, the favourites; the favourites may become clichés, but great poetry can stand up to that. The Bible and Shakespeare are the evidence.

So why not anthologies of words, which may serve as Little Dictionaries, companions for the rest-hour or the railway-train? To meet that need has been my purpose in general. The Great Dictionaries are partly vast because they have to include much with which we need not bother. You can hardly go to Paddington or to bed with the O.E.D. But you can put an anthology in your pocket or on the bed-side table. And that at small expense. (I thank my publisher for managing to keep these books so cheap for so long: a small increase has now to be made, which is no fault of ours. Considering that book-production costs — paper, printing, binding and so on — are about four times what they were when the first of my series appeared in 1942, there is little ground for resenting the small addition.)

My method has not been to go raking through a dictionary or to rely on correspondents, active and generous though the latter have been. I collect words as I read, quote the instances, and then start looking them up and seeing where they lead. They often enchant me not only by their own extraordinary history but by their proximity to another strange specimen. Dictionaries suggest a way-ward piece of exploration in town or country: you start out to see some guide-book favourite, the prescribed 'sight'. But, as you go, all sorts of urban alleys or rustic paths may profitably seduce you to find out the oddities and beauties with which guide-books

6

cannot be bothered. So with words. Hunting out one, you stumble on six more. Nobody who paddles in a dictionary will long be unrewarded. The number of words in everyday use whose origin is unknown to you and may prove to be amusing or exciting is very large. Dictionaries are unfailing servants of that great human virtue, curiosity.

May I remind Scottish readers, and indeed all readers with a friendly concern for variations in dialect, that the *Scottish National Dictionary*, which should do for the rich and diverse vocabulary of that country what Oxford has done for English, still moves slowly? It took a long time to start it and the labours of collection and annotation are very heavy for a small staff of devotees who have never been sufficiently or systematically endowed. At the time of writing this vitally important work has reached Dra-. Only that far. Yet there is a notable revival of Scottish literature in the 'Lallans', which is sister of the 'Hielans' or Gaelic. The Scots language draws on French and Scandinavian as well as on native and Gaelic sources. It is a glorious torrent of vernacular, foamy and richly brown like a burn in spate.

There is, of course, Jamieson and an abridged Jamieson is one of my best companions. But it is dated 1846 and the torrent has swollen since then. It is ridiculous that a nation which annually celebrates Burns as eagerly and constantly as the English celebrate the Cup Final, should be so laggard in arranging its National Gallery of the beauties which Burns, among many others, had used to his advantage and immortalized to ours. Those who are interested should write to the *Scottish National Dictionary* at King's College, Aberdeen, where David Murison and his colleagues shoulder, inadequately assisted, a task as glorious as it is gigantic. Donations, I fancy, will not be refused. But it is not a case of cadging. They have something good to sell, something which no public library and no private one of any size or ambition, especially if the owner be Scottish, should be without.

As a side-line to my commentary on the attractive and amusing words, I have scolded the pretentious lingo of the jargons, especially of Officialese. The years go by and Officialese and all the other -eses remain their ponderous selves. Sir Alan Herbert had ridiculed the pomp of piffle; Dr. Ifor Evans in *The Use of English, a Primer of Direct English* has gone beyond the easy attack, taken abominable examples of tangled pretentious Governmental or Business verbosity, and rewritten them in a sensible and simple way, proving that really it is not impossible for an administrator to be intelligible. Sir Ernest Gowers, writing closer to Whitehall, has also expounded better ways. But I do not notice much improvement. To give short names to little things, to write an Order in terms of common usage, affronts the pride of the minor official. He sees himself as with a high commission and not as other men. So he makes it a part of his dignity, if not of his vanity, to describe a rat-catcher as an Officer with deratizational and deinfestational functions or to compose the instructions to a village grocer in a lingo which might just possibly be comprehended by a lawyer after a whole morning's application to the job of interpretation.

The Public Man, when he writes a letter to the more serious Press, often sets a shocking example of style and rivals the most jaded leader-writer in his parade of dead metaphors. Even when the subject is education, the result may be a warning to pupils. I have a minute or two ago read a communication from an Educational Expert which starts with, 'A tocsin has been sounded'. He omitted to add that this French alarm-bell was fluttering the dove-cots of Whitehall, but those who take up the issue will certainly set the cat among the pigeons as well as visualizing dove-cot perturbations. (If we must have Civil Service dove-cots, why not use the Scottish doo-cot, which murmurs the right drowsy kind of noise?) So we go on exploring our avenues, after the bomb-shell has fallen or the tocsin has sounded, and putting the reader to sleep by the staleness of it all. Who does not yawn at meeting yet another tocsin or bomb-shell (an extinct bell and a non-existent missile) in a call to gird up our loins?

Fortunately Etymology, as professed and expounded in Universities, becomes less pedantic; books on language are frequently issued and seek a popular market in the many and excellent popular series. The indefatigable Eric Partridge toils on at the lexicography of all kinds of speech and charts countless streams of strange and fascinating words. My own corner has been, as I said, that of the anthologist, a compiler of Little Dictionaries, with their personal choices and capricious meanderings of commentary. Those who write to correct or encourage or instruct me have done so from near and far and, as I said, it is they who have chiefly made me break my promise to desist. But the blame is not wholly theirs. It has been a form of self-indulgence to start again, in the odd hours left over from other tasks and forms of writing. It is a change from the solving of crossword puzzles, which, incidentally, bring to notice some bizarre and bewitching terms. To one of casual habits the making of anthologies is attractive because it can be done in the stray half-hours. Perhaps that is why anthologies abound. They may be an idler's way of showing that he is not altogether idle. Finally I express my gratitude to my most recent helpers whose names are

Cecil Andrews
Ian Angus-Wilson
Janet Ashbee

T. Baty
W. T. L. Becker
Moncure Biddle
A. W. Boyd
Philip W. F. Brown
Amy M. Bull

John H. Chaplin
D. B. Chidsey
Mrs. A. M. Clarke
Philip Conklin

J. H. Cosens
William Cox
Dr. C. Willett Cunnington

Dorothy Dainty
John H. Donaldson
A. B. Dutton

F. Edmunson
Monica Ewer

Arthur Garnett
Daniel George

G. Halliday
J. Hely-Hutchinson

9

Daniel Hepburn
J. W. Holme
Patrick Home
Cecil Hull
David Hussey

J. Jamieson

Eiluned Lewis

Mrs. Mary McCredie
Ngaio Marsh
E. F. Meier
Mona Morley

Michael Pearson
Stewart Perowne
Derrick Perritt
W. G. Priest

Arthur Ransome
J. Davis Reichard

Dr. G. K. C. Rettie
William Roberts

J. Leslie Sadler
B. D. Sandwell
H. Dwight Sedgwick
C. Frank Shaw
Theodore Sturgeon
Mary Sturrock

J. W. K. Taylor
H. G. Tempest
Kenneth Thomas
Dr. E. J. Thomson
J. C. Trewin
Stephen Trimen

The late Earl Wavell
Prof. J. W. Williams
Walter L. Williams
Barbara Worsley-Gough

ADIAPHORIST

IN the literature of the seventeenth century you may run into an Adiaphorist, who is one showing indifference in theology; he is not in our sense an indifferent (or incompetent) theologian. Rather does he show an absence of enthusiasm, a word which originally meant divine possession and so was applied to wild forms of fervour. Pepys used the term latitudinarian for the adiaphorist, defining his friend Wilkins, Bishop of Chester, as a rising man because of his latitude in theology. The citizens of Laodicea, who ran a moderate temperature in theological affairs, have been made by one of Thomas Hardy's titles the typical adiaphorists.

I thought that the reference to Laodicean temperance came in 'The Acts of the Apostles'. But Laodicea is chiefly mentioned in the Epistle 'to the saints and faithful brethren which are at Colosse', in which the Colossians are recommended to read 'the epistle from Laodicea'. This is something of a compliment to the latter; the scolding of that place which gave it a name for ever as a home of cold (or rather of tepid) fish, came in 'Revelation'.

> And unto the angel of the church of the Laodiceans write 'These things saith the Amen, the faithful and true witness, the beginning of the creation of God; I know thy works, that thou art neither cold nor hot; I would thou wert cold or hot.
> So then because thou art lukewarm and neither cold nor hot, I will spue thee out of my mouth.

The irate 'Amen' was certainly no adiaphorist in his attitude to adiaphorism and in calling Laodiceans to 'be zealous and repent'. Now there is a cant phrase, wickedly overworked, 'I couldn't care less', to signify indifference in general. Adiaphorism and latitudinarianism have been mainly restricted to theology. But I suppose a man can be called Laodicean about any cult, even about cricket.

ADSCITITIOUS AND BEZZLE

I CAME across this Latinity amid the gay scholarship of Dr. Leslie Hotson's Shakespearean researches. This happy sifter of innumerable Rolls and Registers goes Jack-Hornering in the Record Office and, with his assistants, is generally to be relied upon to pull out a plum. The assumption that nothing more of fact will ever be discovered about Shakespeare is continually dissipated by Dr. Hotson's discoveries among the ancient files: these discoveries may not always be large, but they do link up the elusive dramatist with hitherto unknown figures of the Tudor and Jacobean scene, such as William Johnson, first apprentice and then landlord of the 'Mermaid'. Hitherto there had been no evidence that Shakespeare ever had anything to do with that favourite haunt both of the poets and the 'roaring boys'. Now it is demonstrated that the witness of one of Shakespeare's purchases of property, the Blackfriars Gate-House, was called William Johnson, Vintner. The Chancery records make it plain that the 'Meeremayd' was in the tenure of William Johnson, Vintner. This does not prove that William Shakespeare was a highly absorbent customer of Johnson's or a member of the 'right-generous, jovial, and mercurial Sireniacks' who took their pleasure there with Ben Jonson and the rest. But it does prove the existence of an interesting acquaintance in a life that has aroused and so largely defeated the curiosity of the world.

But I am slow in reaching my words. Adscititious is introduced by Dr. Hotson, who is a word-happy scholar, well dyed in the great vat of historic English verbosity. It means brought in, supplementary, additional. Evelyn the Diarist used it. Is it to be taken up now by youth attempting English style? I fancy that many examiners would be floored by it should they find it in a student's answer: and it is imprudent to be more learned than the judge. However, there it is for those who like to add imposingly to our terms for additional.

Dr. Hotson's zest for adscititious terminology is exemplified in his discussion of London breweries of the reign of Queen Elizabeth in a volume called *Shakespeare's Sonnets Dated*.

Stow remarks, 'the Brewers for the more part remain near to the friendly water of Thames'. Friendly not only because it bore the shipping to Queenhithe and Billingsgate with sea-coal for their furnaces, and stores of hops and hard, straw-dried yellow malt, but also because they used Thames water for their 'liquor'. For in spite of Nashe's observation that brewers grow rich 'by retayling filthy Thames water', that same water was generally held to produce the best beer (Harrison, *Descr. of England*, New Shak. Soc., I. 160). More than that, English beer, with London beer made of filthy Thames water at the head, was so celebrated and sought after that despite the diligent bezzling and beer-bathing of English tosspots, bench-whistlers, and lick-wimbles, 'like dromedaries in the caravana, drinking for the thirst past, for the thirst present, and for the thirst to come', the hard-working brewers of England made enough not only to satisfy the home market, but to supply a large export trade as well.

Here is verbal plenty indeed, sufficiency of toper-names to deserve the epithet of adscititious. Bezzling lick-wimbles, toss-pots, and bench-whistlers made lively company no doubt: and dubious, dangerous company too, if bezzling had then got its secondary meaning which is known to us better in the longer word, embezzle.

To bezzle was to booze and behave sottishly; and, because sots need funds and may snatch at them for lack of will to earn them honestly, a bezzler was one who not only guzzled and soaked but made away with the property of others in order to do so. So we have derived the embezzler, who may, after all, be a fanatical tee-totaller; he is nominally descended from the toss-pots of the Tudor tavern: he is but a lick-wimble gone further down hill. One of the old usages of wimble was as a synonym for nimble and I take a lick-wimble to be a bezzling fellow as ready with his tongue and lips as a dog on a hot day.

HERE is a pleasant adjective that has considerably changed its meaning. It must signify, by derivation, friendly in talk or friendly while being talked at. *O.E.D.* defines it as 'easy of conversation and address, civil and courteous in responding to the conversation of others, especially inferiors or equals'. In short, an epithet for the great who chat easily with the less great. But now it is applied to objects which are by nature deaf and dumb and even to sporting contests.

Here are two sentences taken from the same issue of *The Times*. 'The match between M.C.C. and Queensland ambled affably along towards a draw.' 'The hanging judgment reserved for horses has never popularly been passed on Landseer's affable lions'. The first sentence was applied to a cricket-match, the second to London's statues, neither of which could accurately be described as owners of active tongues and ears. In Shakespeare's much-discussed sonnet about the Rival Poet there is allusion to

> that affable familiar ghost
> Which nightly gulls him with intelligence

and, however we interpret that, we can agree that an affable ghost is an agreeable form of shade. Though not a great believer in angels or their superior officers with the prefix arch-, I have always felt kindly disposed to Raphael since Milton called him 'The affable archangel'. In the first part of *Henry IV* Mortimer says of his father, so disliked of Hotspur:

> In faith, he is a worthy gentleman;
> Exceedingly well-read, and profited
> In strange concealments; valiant as a lion,
> And wondrous affable, and as bountiful
> As mines of India.

So we come back to the lions, beasts affable, according to *The Times*, at least in the graven images designed by the good Sir Edwin, but only valiant to Shakespeare, who limited his attributions of affability, and rightly, to articulate ghosts and other masters of the spoken word. It is a nice adjective for the good mixer and ready man at a party, but surely we have stretched it rather far when we affix it to a dull cricket match, which neither promises nor provides a result, and to animals cut in stone.

ALLAGRUGOUS

THE leading companions of Prince Charles Edward Stuart, who sailed with him in July 1745 and helped to raise the standard at Glenfinnan, were sometimes known as the Seven Men of Moidart and have naturally been idealized as heroes of a forlorn hope. They were tersely described by a Mr. Bissatt of Blair Atholl as 'old allagrugous like fellows as ever I saw'. 'Allagrugous is interpreted to mean grim', added Andrew Lang when quoting Bissatt. Jamieson's *Scottish Dictionary* confirms the idea of ghastliness with learned allusion to a source 'Moeso-Gothic as preserved in the Uphilas Version of the Gospels'. I am totally ignorant of the Moeso-Goths and of the Uphilas Bible too, but I agree that allagrugous is a good word for those who want to be impolite about grim and ghastly fellows.

AMBIVALENCE

HERE is a vogue-word of recent appearance. It does not appear at all in my two-volume *O.E.D.* A long-established Scottish-English Dictionary, that of the house of Chambers, knew nothing of it until its most recent edition when it admitted the term with the bracketed explanation (Psych), suggesting that some psychologist hath done this. Psychology is now a leader in word-making and journalists use ambivalent with a wide variety of meanings. It should, apparently, signify possessing contrasted emotional states, but it is applied to such notions as neutrality and facing both ways. Even sex-and-murder novelists now have it on their list of favourites. Here is an extract from *Something for Nothing* by H. Vernon Dixon, a tale of a beautiful racketeer at large among the Californian rich; it is a fiction on which every vice has its grip. 'She threw herself about and into his arms and clung to him fiercely. "You're no good," she whispered, "but I'm crazy about you. I loathe you and I — I guess I love you too. There's a word for it — ambivalence".' To this display of erudition by the amorous lady the terse and masculine answer was 'Yeah'.

The lady later remarked, somewhat unnecessarily, that she was 'all wild and physical' and that she had no shame. To which the racketeer replied, with good sense but something less than courtesy, 'Stop yapping'. No ambivalence about that. He believed in the deeds of love rather than in lavish concessions to its psychological terminology. But why blame him? He was in the highest and most reverend literary company. Dr. John Donne, destined Dean of St. Paul's, had given quite as vigorous expression to the 'Stop yapping' sentiments of Mr. Dixon's libidinous racketeer when he began a poem to a lady, 'For God's sake, hold your tongue and let me love.'

But Donne and the poets who followed him were subject to much emotional ambivalence, though they lacked that lingo for it. I gather from all this that when the Roman Catullus wrote '*Odi et amo*' (I hate and love) he should have signed himself '*Ambivalens*'. J. B. Priestley, with his nice appreciation of verbal vogues, properly introduced ambivalence into the works of the poet-lecturer, Mr. Grope, who was imposed upon the culture-hungry minority of Farbridge in his recent novel *Festival at Farbridge*. After offering,

All the vanilla avenues,
With blood on the blinds,
Are closed
To centaurs
And leading technicians in small bicycle
                                    factories.

When shall we meet
Flamingoes in the maze?

Mr. Grope proceeded to recite

Undulating circumstances
And the tired funeral
Of my oldest aunt,
Who had always wondered about Turkestan,
Brought ambivalence,
No consternation,
But sugar, if you don't mind.

Surely this is no exaggeration of the verbal antics of the Gibberish
and Spasmodist schools, so long acclaimed by the passionate few.

AMERCE

WHEN I was a boy I read the beginning of Conington's version
of *The Aeneid*.

Arms and the man I sing who first
From realm of Ilium amerced.

I was puzzled by amerced. It was obviously 'poetese' for separated
or exiled. Conington was, I suppose, echoing Milton's 'amerced
of heaven'. But amercement is properly fining. If you are fined a
pound, you are separated from it.

I was surprised to see the old amerced turning up in modern journalism. The Journal of the Commons, Open Spaces, and Footpaths Preservation Society, made this inquiry.

> Since ramblers are simply members of the public who enjoy country walks and already make their appropriate contribution to the rates and taxes out of which the expense of repairing highways (including public paths) is met, why should they in particular be amerced for using paths which every citizen has a legal right to use?

Amerce, in the financial sense, was commonly employed by the writers of our Romantic Revival. But, since poetry now prefers conversational idioms, it is unlikely to turn up in modern verse. However, it has still a niche in leader-writer's English, which has a lingo of its own and is indeed often rich in the relics of romanticism. Who would say, over the breakfast table, 'It bids fair to be a wet day and it behoves you take your mackintosh.' Yet leader-writers are continually concerned with these fair bids. They are also continually involved in 'behoviour'. All sorts of evil things 'bid fair' to become national scandals or liabilities which it behoves us to avert. I rank amercement with behoving or bidding fair. Nobody would tell his wife that he had been amerced for parking his car in a disparked area. But he might read that the amercement of citizens for such trifling offences bids fair to become tyrannical.

ANTIPERASTASIS

I MENTION this Grecian mouthful meaning 'contrast of circumstance' not to recommend it, but because of its occurence in a lyric; one would expect to find it in a medical or philosophical treatise. Concerning the senile ambition of Anacreon to remain a lover, Abraham Cowley wrote,

Love was with thy life entwined
Close as heat with fire is joined,
A powerful brand prescribed the date
Of thine, like Meleager's fate.
Th' antiperastasis of age
More enflamed thy amorous rage.

Not a good poem, not a good word. But a reminder that join was long pronounced jine and that poets of the second class may be pedants of the first order.

AVAILABILITY

HERE is a fine word for Officialese, in which plenty and scarcity are unknown. 'The availability of 18-inch pipes is practically negligible' (announcement of a Public Works Department) is good Barnacular bunkum for the news that such pipes are very scarce. That master of bureaucratic procedure who wrote 'This is not a technical survey, but a survey to find out what surveys are necessary' was probably much hampered by 'negligible availability of personnel'.

The opposite of negligible availability is redundancy. Redund (or redound) abides though not, as a rule, with its first meaning of overflowing; the Latin *unda*, a wave, is the base of both words. Nowadays Redound is mainly applied to praiseworthy matters. 'Redound to your credit' has become a cliché. The adjective redundant, on the other hand, has a note of censure and displeasure, being common Officialese for too many. It is especially applied to public-houses and saloons by their enemies, when these establishments are of 'high availability'. Recently a verb 'reduntantize' has appeared; this atrocity means, presumably, to create excess. I can imagine some gaunt tycoon of Welfare announcing to the world that 'opportunities for the consumption of liquor in this area, though recently of negligible availability, have now been reduntantized by the inadvertent granting of supernumerary licences, a policy which should certainly be reviewed by the appropriate authorities when they conduct the next sociological survey of regional community life among the underprivileged brackets'.

BALD

T H E R E is a puzzle about bald. Did it mean white first and hairless later? Bald patches and skulls, with darkly hirsute environs, can look surprisingly white. A bald actor's skull gleams moon-bright on a spot-lit or a flood-lit stage; that is why actors, when going 'a bit thin on top', prefer to wear toupées. It is not the sparsity of thatch that worries them. It is the way in which theatrical lighting underlines it, so that a spectator in the gallery, looking down on the head rather than the face, may regard a bald actor as a beacon walking. Of course to a certain kind of comedian this surface gleam is an asset; the late Alfred Drayton and his partner in wild nonsense Robertson Hare gained hugely by their radiant domes, but, in the case of a juvenile lead, it is not so pleasant to have the absence or the blanching of one's locks thus heavily emphasized by electricity. The Americanism 'balding' is now common in English fiction and journalism.

The case for bald being originally white is strengthened by reference to zoology. The Bald-Faced Stag of America is so called after a white patch; so are Bald-Coot, Bald-Eagle and Bald-Buzzard. And our adjective pie-bald, linking with mag-pie, certainly suggests whiteness rather than hairlessness in a horse. Skew-bald, also, does not refer to absence of coat but to a parti-coloured coat, sometimes sorrel and white. There seems to be a fairly strong case for believing that, in the history of the word bald, the colour came before the falling of the locks. *Chambers Dictionary* says of bald 'Originally, "shining", "white", from the Irish and Gaelic bàl, a white spot'. But *Chambers* also accepts the curious possibility that the bald man was so called because he had a smooth head like a ball. A bare, round-topped mountain in the Highlands is usually called Maol. Of course the greater Maols are frequently gleaming white with snow as well as with the summer shine of naked rock.

To this kind of Maol Matthew Arnold sensibly likened William Wordsworth. 'His expression may often be called bald . . . but it is bald as the mountain-tops are bald, with a baldness full of grandeur.'

On the baldness of speech we can quote Pooh-Bah in *The Mikado*. 'Merely corroborative detail intended to give verisimilitude to an otherwise bald and unconvincing narrative.' The polysyllabic dismissal has lingered. 'Bald and unconvincing narrative' has become a cliché and a jest. But a tale untrimmed and even naked is surely more likely to convince than one which has been given a shampoo and generally frizzed up by the narrator; word-spinning can be a form of 'hair-do' and, like hair-dos, it may be deceptive.

BARTIZAN

CONSTRUCTORS of fortification had a taste for the letter 'b'. I find bartizan a sonorous and imposing form of battlement or tower; Sir Walter Scott's mind moved powerfully amid bartizan-ning. Bartizan 'a small overhanging turret projecting from the angle on top of a tower' was a superflux of baronial turretry and some of those Victorian Scottish merchants who ploughed their profits into stone — if such a thing is possible — in the form of neo-baronial castles in the Highlands had a quenchless appetite for bartizans. Brattice, a temporary breast-work, belongs to this school of Balmoralist medievalism. I cannot think of barbizans without barbicans: these are outer-fortifications, especially over a gate or bridge, serving as a watch-tower. And barbicans inevitably remind me of barbecues; these are culinary, not structural, being very large grills or gridirons and also signifying the purposes they serve, i.e. large picnics at which animals are cooked whole. That too has a medieval sound to us, but not to Australians. Our Test Match teams are entertained, up country, to barbecues and may, or may not, bat and bowl all the better thereafter.

BEJEZEBELLED

I WAS reading C. E. Montague on Oscar Wilde and approving his view that

> Wilde, like Disraeli, showed a strain, perhaps irremediable, of second-rateness in the craving of his imagination for curious, bedizened, exotic, or abnormal stuff to work on. Unlike the greatest imaginations, which are always making some old and plain thing new again, Wilde's is always seeking refuge in strange places from its own inability to do this: and as every step in this flight from the trite increases the trodden area, he was always driven farther and farther into paradox and absurdity.

Reflecting on the truth of that, I remembered an adjective used by James Agate, bejezebelled. Wilde's verbiage in *Salome* went beyond bedizenment. It was bejezebelled, a luscious essay in the art of seducing callow minds by flaunting a fictitious beauty. But there was another prose of Wilde's, and a worthier.

BERLINE

BERLIN, before it added much to the worst of Germany's mind and methods, had contributed quite nicely to our vocabulary, giving us woollens, carriages and boots. The berline, a hooded and roomy vehicle for long travel, always figures in the lives of Bonnie Prince Charles, because it was in this type of conveyance that his mother, Princess Clementine Sobieska, was smuggled out of her convent in Silesia to marry, not very happily, 'poor old Mr. Melancholy', as the Hanoverians called the good and gloomy Old Pretender. The Captain Wogan who led the escapade and told his own story in a pamphlet called *French Fortitude*, 'printed in London for the Entertainment of the Curious', had with him four Irish officers and a Mrs. Missett to chaperone the Princess (good name for a duenna!) They travelled in a 'strong Coach, able to stand the Shock of so great a Journey and a Melancholy Variety of ugly Accidents'. The berline did, in fact, break down, but a waggon assisted the flight and took them to Bologna. The intended bridegroom had gone off to Spain and there was, unromantically, a marriage by proxy. Thus Scotland, through Irish ingenuity and a berline, got its over-slandered, over-worshipped, brave, unlucky hero of the Forty-Five.

Berlin wool was a Victorian favourite: Berliners as boots were late Georgian. I presume that they were cousins to the Hessians, in which according to the song in *Patience* lovers' confessions are ubiquitously eloquent. That most agreeable sketch by Boz 'The Tuggses at Ramsgate' includes a Berlin-booted episode among the evening diversions in the sea-side 'library'. 'Who's this?' inquired Mr. Cyril Tuggs of Mrs. Captain Waters as a short female in a blue velvet hat and feathers was led into the orchestra by a fat man in black tights and cloudy Berlins. 'Mrs. Tippins of the London theatres', replied Belinda, referring to the programme. Mrs. Tippins (of the London theatres) then sang 'Bid me discourse', after which her 'tighted' and booted squire rendered a comic song and their daughter gave 'an air with variations on the guitar'. One feels that the Berlins added considerably to the genteel artistic effect, just as lion-tamers would be lesser gentlemen (or ladies) without their patent-leather 'tops'.

In the matter of boots and shoes men have exactly reversed Victorian practice. Then the elegant male displayed his boots, while the rougher worker wore shoes. In another essay 'Boz' describes Scotland Yard on its upward social climb from a coal-depot, drawing on the Thames barges, to the housing of considerable shops and even Police Commissioners. The old dark wainscotted inn, serving pints of Barclay's best to the coal-heavers, became Wine-vaults, with a gold-lettered superscription, and a bootmaker took up a tenancy near by, 'exposing for sale boots —

real Wellington boots — an article which a few years ago none of the original inhabitants had seen or heard of'. Doubtless he could show Hessians and Berliners too. In any case boots were strong tokens of the Yard's progress, social and economic.

It is noticeable in *Dombey and Son* that Mr. Toots, that darling fop, was most precise about his boots, whereas, when the great Dombey mansion was sold up, part of the mess was the trail of the porters' muddy shoes as they carted the rich furnishings away. The decay of boots, as examples of shining glory, was completed in Edwardian times when 'low shoes' became fashionable. Convenience in the lacing and lack of leather during two wars and two peace-times of scarcity have confirmed the victory of the masculine shoe for all save military and sporting purposes. So passed Berline and Berlins!

BIFFIN

B O F F I N S came recently to our aid during the wars in back-rooms and laboratories. Biffins are an older stay of the English. 'A baked apple flattened in the form of a cake', says the dictionary. Substantial stuff, surely, since it appears in a farm-house bill of fare in John Moore's *Dance and Skylark*, a tale of Festival high jinks in the 'Elmbury' country of which he writes so richly. 'To this table in their appointed season came Aylesbury ducklings, turkeys, geese, fat capons, rook-pie, pigs' fry and faggots, lambs' tails and such time-honoured delicacies as frumenty, biffins, lardy-cakes, sparrib-pie, love-in-disguise, fairings and ginger-bread husbands. There was always a bowl of cream big enough to drown a cat in and a Double Gloucester cheese the size of a grindstone and without fail on Christmas Day Mrs. Pargetter made three dozen Christmas Puddings just as her mother and her grandmother had done before her.' Frumenty is wheat boiled in milk and spiced. Biffins I have defined. The rest I leave to the greedy imagination.

John Moore was not writing of the Great Exhibition Year, 1851, but of the strictly rationed year, 1951, when John Bull became, by compulsion, almost a vegetarian. His so-called sausages were made of dried milk! Haven't they heard of Fair Shares and Food Narks (Enforcement Officers) down in Elmbury, which is easily identifiable as a town of the Cotswold Fringe?

BISHOP

I H A V E commented before on the astonishing number of meanings belonging to the verb to bishop. It means to confirm a member of the church, to appoint to a bishopric, to let milk burn while cooking, to murder by drowning and to file and tamper with the teeth of a horse in order to make him look younger than he is. A pretty parcel of definition!

In Scots it is 'to beat down earth or stones'. In Charles Murray's 'The Miller Explains' the poem begins,

> The byword 'as sweer as the Miller'
> Disturbs me but little, for hech!
> Ye'll find for ane willin' to bishop
> A score sittin' ready to pech.

Sweer is idle and to pech is to puff and pant. Admirable is the Miller's final defence of his criticized absorption,

> An' sae, man, I canna help thinkin'
> The neighbours unkindly; in truth,
> Afore they can judge o' my drinkin'
> They first maun consider my drooth.

I have no answer to that logic.

BISSON

THE First Player in *Hamlet* describes the mobled queen as threatening the flames of captured Troy with 'bisson rheum', which presumably mean blinding moisture. Bisson means short-sighted or causing to be short-sighted and Shakespeare used it again in the first sense. 'What harm can your bisson conspecuities glean out of this character?' asked Menenius of the Tribunes in *Coriolanus*. Menenius was a prolific wordman and may have been drawing a little on Shakespeare's son-in-law, Dr. John Hall, when he observed (for no particular reason) 'the most sovereign prescription in Galen is but empiricutic'. Did Dr. Hall treat patients for 'bisson conspecuity'? Bisson is an apt term for the eye-stickiness of the waking sleeper. Shakespeare had other things to say about the optical troubles of age. Hamlet told Polonius of old men's eyes 'purging thick amber and plum-tree gum', a poet's relentless description of acute conjunctivitis and discharge. Polonius was becoming bisson.

BLACKGUARD

WE have suffered from Black Shirts in our time and blackguardly, in our sense, many of the wearers did become. But the word has a mild origin. For Swift a blackguard was a shoe-black. He preserved your ebony shine. He had begun life in the middle-ages as a kitchen-scullion who was supposed to clean the pots, pans and iron-ware. He became a military servant or batman; later he was a real soldier, a guardsman in a black uniform. Then came the transition to vagabondage of a criminal kind, with the consequent use of a verb, first to act as a blackguard and later to abuse for blackguardly conduct. The poets have not forgotten the blackguard. In 'Don Juan' *arcades ambo* is translated as 'blackguards both', which is surely giving the rustic rogue rather more villainy than is his due. Clough worked 'sesquipedalian blackguard' into one of his hexameters and Housman's

> We for a certainty are not the first
> Have sat in taverns while the tempest hurled
> Their hopeful plans to emptiness, and cursed
> Whatever brute and blackguard made the world

is well known and sometimes cited against him as voicing a violent and crude atheism. But he is talking of the cup-shot man who is angrily basing on his own bad luck a general indictment of the scheme of things. He need not be blackguarded for that.

BONUSABLE AND DISINCENTIVE

I AM asked to censure the second word, justly applied to the oppressive taxation which treats honest work honestly declared as a form of vice meriting the most severe mulcting and punitive affliction at the hands of the State. Officialese has surely done much worse. I am also asked to deplore 'bonusable' for those qualified to claim a bonus, be it additional wages or extra payment from profits. I have never understood why a bonus should be masculine. It is as material as a pocketful of coppers. As in *Summum bonum* it should be neuter and its acknowledged recipients therefore bonumable persons. The official excuse for these words is that they save time and money too, especially where wires and cables have to be sent. Dehospitalize has been so justified and I suppose bonusable could be also defended thus. 'Men to whom bonuses are due' (or, as I would pedantically have it, bonums or bona) is certainly cumbrous. Bonusable men is handier, if convenience be the test. It sounds well enough too. 'The fervent toil of bonusable men' amplifies, in modern terms, Vergil's *fervet opus*.

Returning to disincentive, I think it should be called discentive. Incentive is really a musical term; it is that which sets the tune and so braces, encourages, or provokes. Why keep the 'in' when the meaning is altered? A discentor, as opposed to an incentor, would be one who sings against a thing, not a minstrel who pleads for it. But when the prefix 'dis' is placed in front of words already having the prefix 'in', the 'in' is often illogically retained. Why disimpassioned and disimprisoned? Disinfect will pass, because 'fect' by itself means nothing. But I stand for dispassioned and the disprisoning of those whose discentives to hard and honest work have led them into trouble.

BOUGEE

Ben Jonson used bouge of food; presumably the word came from the French bouche. A child, bulging with bouge, seems well described so. A correspondent has called my attention to bougee, a navvy's word for grout. He thinks that the many British labourers engaged in making railway tunnels in France brought it over; the contractors have now taken it from the navvies and it is used still to signify grouting in tunnels. To grout is to fill up gaps with liquid mortar and cement.

'Grout, incidentally, was a slang word for toil when I was an undergraduate. Does it survive? It could be applied to labours of the mind or body. On the hills a climb would be a 'hell of a grout'; in one's rooms a classical text would elicit the same comment. Bougee would also well express the call to ardours and endurances. Is not the ascent of Ben Nevis a considerable bougee? There are plenty of books, which one is supposed to have read, meriting the same term.

BOWSER

N GAIO MARSH reminds me of the Antipodean taste for -owser. The over-Puritanical fuss-pot, for ever endeavouring to interfere with the drinking or sociable habits of others, is a wowser. A bowser is not a human boozer, but a petrol-pump. Then there is the dowser who divines the hidden water-spring. The suggestion is that -owser and liquids are inseparable company. Well, I could add that a carouser, who is a bit of a souser, has just hospitably said 'Now, sir!' and poured me out a rouser. But I see no logical link in these syllabic coincidences.

The same correspondent asks why an Englishman, 'down under', is known as a Pommy and a small farmer as a Cockatoo. The owner of a milk-farm is a cow-cocky. I have no reply.

BUBUKLE

I N Fluellen's famous description of Bardolph's face, 'all bubukles and whelks and flames of fire', the first term is reasonably explained as a telescoping of bubo and carbuncle. Bubo (hence bubonic plague) is a swelling or abscess in the groin or arm-pit. Carbuncles are too painfully familiar to need explanation; they began as red stones, 'anciently spinels or rubies'.

The 'marine mastropod mollusc' called a whilk by Dr. Johnson and now more commonly whelk was not applied to pimples and pustules only by Shakespeare. The usage is as old as Chaucer. The 'sawcefleem Somonour' (pimpled Summoner of offenders), lecherous as a sparrow, suffered thus. Children feared his visage.

> Ther nas quyk-silver, lytarge, ne brymstoon,
> Boras, ceruce, ne oille of Tartre noon,
> Ne oynement that wolde clense and byte,
> That hym myghte helpen of the whelkes white,

Nor of the knobbes sittynge on his chekes.
Wel loved he garleek, oynons, and eek lekes,
And for to drynken strong wyn, reed as blood;
Thanne wolde he speke, and crie as he were wood.

Wood means mad. Probably it was less painful to have white whelks than red carbuncles and bubukles. The wretched Bardolph had the knobby lot; probably his taste in vegetables and in liquor were those of the Somonour, but the blood-red wine would at least be momentary comfort of the body and the spirit for such affliction of the skin.

CAPER

CAPER was short for capriole: this was applied to 'a high leap made by a horse without advancing' and then to human skips and pirouettes of all kinds. 'We that are true lovers run into strange capers' said Touchstone and capers have now become a popular term for any kind of gaiety or nonsense. The word, with its goatish suggestion, is picturesque and useful. It went once with the antics of an Aguecheek: now with what Dr. Johnson called a frisk about the town. As 'a shrub of trailing habit' the other caper is the usual trimming of a dull joint. Its presence with a boiled leg of mutton was mentioned as 'the trimmings' by Mr. Weller at the Bath 'swarry' of gentlemen's gentlemen. Its dearth was also mourned by the solemn Dr. Ogden in a story told by 'Evidences' Paley and taken by W. Clarke Russell for his *Book of Table Talk*. There was question of a recent meal in the country. To the reply 'Nothing but a boiled leg of mutton', Ogden 'subjoined with a cadence as if concluding a sentence in delivering a sermon, "No capers!"' I like the gravity of 'subjoined', a ponderous word for 'added', but one perhaps proper to a caperless universe.

CHAGRIN

FRET meant gnaw, erode, break down, long before it meant worry. Chagrin is another word which began with the physical and was transferred to the emotional. Chagrin is a form of Shagreen, rough, grained leather. The name of the article was transferred to the irritation it produced. The Middle Eastern horse-dealers used to treat their hides by pressing seeds into them which, after various scrapings and soakings, produced granulation on the surface. Why take all this trouble to turn a smooth leather into one so rough that its name has come to denote pain and mortification? (The latter is yet another of those words which have passed from the body to the soul.) Presumably the pimply and pain-giving leather was the more durable.

I had thought that Shagreen was applied only to the skin of the shark, but, while it now has that special significance, it came originally from the horses and asses of Turkestan and Araby. It is usually dyed green, but might as well be purple or black; as chagrin, in its later meaning of pained resentment, it is at least half or even whole mourning for an injury or an insult. The word has a French look and, before I learned about the sharks and the horses, I had a vague idea that it must be of French origin. But it appears that, even in matters of emotional laceration, there is 'nothing like leather'.

I came across chagrin meaning grief and spelled shagreen in a touching letter sent by Denis O'Dea, an Irish soldier of fortune serving in the Neapolitan army, to the King of France after the early death of Prince Charles Edward Stuart's illegitimate daughter by Clementina Walkinshaw, Charlotte Duchess of Albany. It is printed in Henrietta Tayler's life of *Prince Charlie's Daughter*.

I am certain your Majesty will receive many and many compliments in the death of the respectfull Duchess of Albany, but can boldly say that mine are of the most sincere both by duty and true inclination. I therefore condole with your majesty with a true Irish heart in this very disagreeable subject on which you don't find proper to enlarge, for not to renew your just shagreen and mine.

Your Majesty's most devoted humble
servant and faithful subject
Denis o'Dea

O'Dea used curious English, but his letter is worth far more than are many of the correct formalities which mourning may produce.

CHIFFONIER

A CHIFFONIER was a French rag-gatherer; it was also a cupboard or a side board. Do we have the article still? Or rather do we preserve the name with its Norman and seigneurial ring? In seaside lodgings, perhaps. For it was on the North Shore of Blackpool that Haslam Mills, so exact as well as so witty in his picturing of the grey pastures of Victorian Lancashire, in his boyhood discovered each year behind a frosted glass and amid a blizzard of circulars from the Wesleyan Chapel and the Winter Garden, the 'apartments' of his young felicity. There was 'The Woman of Samaria' in oleograph. 'The cupboard in the chiffonier emitted a powerful odour of Madeira cake and from the floor below there ascended a tinkling of crockery coupled with the exudations of something frying which was not for us.'

That kind of lodging-house has had to stand the competition of holiday-camps with their brisk communal life, but Blackpool is not easily overwhelmed. Were I to conduct a search for England's noblest cruet standing on the most shiny and imposing chiffonier, I would still make a start among the Oakdenes and Glengarries of the North Shore and hope to find yet again that powerful odour of Madeira cake.

CIRCUMORBITAL

CIRCUMLOCUTION marches on: or, if not circumlocution, polysyllabic Latinity. One of the triumphs of modern education has been to bring a bandaged policeman into a Birmingham police-court where he explained, from under his swaddlings, that he was suffering from circumorbital haematoma, in other words, as George Robey would have sung in the old days, a black eye. The brief report of what this scholarly diagnostician deposed went no further. I can only hope that the wounded witness did not fail to attribute his mutilated 'mince pie', as one of his vulgar Cockney colleagues might have called it, to 'a fearful concatenation of circumstances'. Circumorbital haematoma deserved no less.

CLICK

DURING the 1914-18 war click was a common term for 'getting-off' or picking, or being picked, up. 'Did you click last night?' But sex-slang is oddly evanescent. Just as the spooners and mashers had vanished by then, so the clickers had disappeared before the next great war. I made some inquiries as to the survival of click and got an affirmative from Wales and negatives elsewhere. Another word which I hardly ever hear now is flirt. Harsher terms seem now to be employed where our seniors would have called a girl a flirt. The Elizabethan flirt-gill, used by Shakespeare and Ben Jonson for the clickers of their time, is defined as a mixture of flirt and Juliana. (I had not realized that Gill or Jill was Juliana.) But flirting except in its original sense of rapid movement, as of a bird's wings and feathers, is chiefly of the nineteenth century. The click episcopal was discovered by Sydney Smith. 'How can a bishop flirt?' he inquired, 'the most he can say is, "I will see you in the vestry after service".' Lord Chesterfield had earlier asserted that 'I assisted at the birth of that most significant word flirtation, which dropped from the most beautiful mouth in the world'. But the term flirt, deemed innocent by Byron, was a word much favoured by the Victorians; use of it censored, but it did not finally condemn.

COMFORTABLY

THE common use of the adverb comfortably to mean easily can result in some surprising judgments. A medical witness went into the box at a particularly revolting murder-trial. The corpse had been sliced up for concealment. The doctor laid it down in giving his evidence that 'A human body could be cut up comfortably in about an hour'.

COMMODIOUS

WE are accustomed now to finding commodious used as a solemn term for spacious in the advertisements of Estate Agents. Premises are commodious, houses 'standing in their own grounds' are 'commodious and desirable residences'. Commodious has long hovered between the dubiously profitable and the admirably ample. The Bastard's famous speech in *King John* makes commodity a form of cunning policy.

> That smooth-faced gentleman, tickling Commodity,
> Commodity, the bias of the world . . .
> This bawd, this broker, this all-changing word,

and he ends with the frank confession

> Since kings break faith upon commodity,
> Gain be my lord, for I will worship thee.

There is no merit about commodious there.

Yet Milton could describe the ample opportunities of a University career as 'a commodious life' spent among 'those courteous and learned men', the Fellows of his College.

The commode, as a noun, was familiar as a bedroom commodity, in the sense of useful article, and was also a tire for the heads of ladies, a wire-frame with lace adornings. The Huguenot Mountjoy, with whom we know that Shakespeare lodged in Silver Street, was a craftsman of such tires or commodes. To enter the room with a commode on her head was not for Queen Elizabeth or Nell Gwynne a display of music-hall acrobatics. They knew their commodious bedroom furniture as joint-stools. Commode seems to have been a Victorian nicety of term.

COMPLAISANCE

I N 1776 the English traveller Topham visited Edinburgh; his views of the Scots were considerably more genial than those of Dr. Johnson. 'I know of no quality more conspicuous in the inhabitants than complaisance, which is common to every age and sex, but more particularly to the women who seem to make it a study to oblige.' He found excellence everywhere. Good breeding, enchanting accomplishments, beauty unexcelled, minds as well ornamented as the bodies — all were there. He poured compliments in a most complaisant manner, as he understood complaisance, namely as politeness and good manners. Of the peasants he was no less appreciative. Instead of the 'stubborn rudeness, shyness and barbarism', which he discovered in the English village, he found 'a compliant obsequiousness, softness of temper, an ambition to oblige, and sociability' in the Scottish countryside. Not all English travellers have been so liberal in praise — or may I, as a Scot, say so discriminating?

It is odd that Topham, in his liberality of praise for a Caledonia supposedly stern and wild, should have used two words both or which have changed their meaning for the worse. Complaisance, which was courtesy, has become complacence, which is very nearly as bad as self-righteousness. Complacence is now most commonly applied to laziness or foolishness which will not admit its own sloth or folly, while obsequiousness has become a fawning humility of a hateful kind. Originally the obsequious man was one who observed the rites and duties of his office; the poets called the punctual sun obsequious in the skies. Obsequies, in the plural, are burial rites and one of those 'flight-words' whereby we seek not to see plain the grim realities. Naturally death has evoked many of such evasions. People who pass away have the obsequies of interment: they do not just die and get buried. The funeral party becomes a cortège. Death has its verbal pomp indeed.

It is a pity that the happy word complaisance should have disappeared into the ugly qualities of the complacent man. In recent years something of Topham's affection for Scottish manners has been well-earned. While many a traveller was grumbling at the brusqueness and brashness of Londoners when it came to any matter of service, there was often a tribute to the 'complaisance', in the old meaning, of Scottish hospitality and of the Scottish caterers for the stranger in their midst.

COVEN

THE word convent is now used mainly of religious buildings; but it is, in origin, an assembly of persons, not the place of assembly. Very often it was an assembly of twelve, similar in number to the fellowship of the Apostles, or of thirteen, if the Leader be included. There could be convents of merchants as well as those dedicated to a faith. I do not think there was ever a convent of witches. For them we have reserved a shorter form of the same word, coven. A coven of witches was a covey of thirteen, as we would say of other flighty fowl. I wondered whether the sportsman's covey might not be yet another form of convent or coven, meaning a group. But it is attributed by the dictionaries to the French couvée, a brood, a hatching.

The Scots were especially interested in the covens of the broom-stick-riders. A coven or covine of witches was the Deil's Dozen, a band of thirteen of whom two were officials, the Maiden of the Coven and the Officer who called the roll. The Maiden was seated next the Devil himself. Those two led the dance very formidably called Gillatrypes. This is not a bad name for a hags' hop.

The Latin verb *convenire*, to come together, has given us the convent, the coven and the covine which is what bad convents (in the sense of assemblies) might come to, namely a plot. In *Redgauntlet* you may read of one 'deboshed with brandy through the device, counsel, and covyne of another'.

Then there was the covin-tree, under which, particularly in Scotland, the owner of a house met his 'convent' of visitors or saw them off. In front of any old Scottish mansion there is usually a big tree, a fine larch perhaps, where these greetings took place. Apparently it was more polite to be out of doors when hailing honoured guests or bidding them farewell. As rain is not unknown outside Scottish country-houses, the coven-tree had its use as a major umbrella for sheltering these ceremonial conventions.

A covenant is a coming-together of strong opinions and of resolute wills, as well as a legal agreement and pledge. Scotland has been a great nurse unto this day of covenants and Covenanters. Indeed, that country makes a wide use of the Latin verb *convenire* and its derivatives. The chairman of a committee or council is its convener and Scottish Convention is the assembly of Scottish Home Rulers. A group of Scottish Nationalists might be called, by their opponents and others who do not like to see ancient relics spirited out of Westminster Abbey, 'a coven of Covenanters'.

Conventicle is a diminutive assembly or a small place of meeting, and the allusion to littleness has conveyed a sneer. Christians have often been sadly uncharitable in their attitude to a rival creed or sect; they have tried to demean a cause by derision of its housing.

37

Conventicles are the opposite of cathedrals, but conventicleers or conventiculists have been ready to suffer in the extreme for their meeting-house, whatever its lack of size or modesty of architecture.

COWTEREER

'HE's one of those cowtereers,' said the girl in the Tube surveying the portrait of male elegance. She was referring to a dress-maker, whom nowadays you must not call anything so common as that. He — since the males have usurped the sovereignty of the craft — is a couturier, and no longer even a costumier. Costumiers went out when the trade decided that the word costume should be limited to a lady's suit. But surely the great Lucille would not have minded being a costumier in her day.

In my paper I read, 'Couturiers' preoccupation with tweed is reflected in quantities of small-check outfits'. I suppose this means 'The tweed-fashion is producing many small-check outfits'. There is the abiding shortage of news-print; there are tiny papers. Yet all the time precious lines are wasted because journalists will not make a plain statement. The preoccupied cowtereer with a flow of small-check outfits as the result of his reflections is a fascinating specimen.

In order to look brisk and curt the writer dropped 'the' before Couturiers. I get very weary of this un-articled English. If brevity be essential it is ridiculous to save three letters and then waste thirty by drifting off into pompous periphrases about preoccupations and such like.

CRAVAT

THE Cravat was originally a piece of Croatian neckware, sometimes of lace. I would think of it, more recently, as a large, showy kind of neck-tie, but to Conan Doyle and Sherlock Holmes it was a muffler. 'It was a wild tempestuous night towards the close of November. Outside the wind howled down Baker Street while the rain beat fiercely against the windows.' The inevitable cab came down the empty street. Enter 'that promising young detective', Stanley Hopkins, to whom Holmes showed a sympathy rarely granted to others of Scotland Yard. Hopkins was introducing the case of *The Golden Pince-nez*. 'My poor Watson,' cried Holmes, scenting immediate work on the pince-nez trail, 'we want overcoats and cravats and goloshes.'

Fifty years later the Cravat of this kind has been much on view, worn without overcoat or goloshes by the Student Class. To wear a school, club, or college scarf or muffler, thrown about the neck is, I suppose, economy's bow to foppery. The student of 1951 cannot afford the fine feathers once available, on long and ample credit, in University towns. The 'fancy vest' has made a brief reappearance, chiefly in buff; but those who want to 'peacock it a bit' find that ties and mufflers — the Holmesian cravats — are the easiest and cheapest means with which to show one's colours. They are sported without relevance to weather. On the coldest days I have seen undergraduates at large and even watching football-matches with no overcoat; they only wreathe the throat with what some of our fathers called, as well as a cravat, a comforter. This same garment is also visibly favoured in days of considerable warmth. The muffler now is a ubiquitous and an all-weather decoration as well as a thoracic defence. But does anybody call it a cravat?

Holmes was fond of writing monographs on this or that obscure topic — indeed, he was unravelling a palimpsest when Hopkins came in from the hurricane and the deluge — and many a monograph has been written upon him. Has any such treatise been written on his use of the English language? His conversational prose was formal and orotund; he loved a cliché as dearly as he loved tobacco and once, alas, cocaine. (But his creator cured him of the last.) How many a case did he describe 'as not entirely devoid of interest'! How often did he say to one of his more distressed clients, 'Pray compose yourself', and even to his life-long ally and companion — can the solid Victorian Watson be called a 'buddy'? — 'Pray, continue'! Indeed, it is with something of a shock that we find the latest Holmes of all — him of *The Retired Colourman* — suddenly snapping at Watson, with no 'pray' at all, 'Cut out the poetry!' Watson's poetry had been no more than the description of a garden-wall in Lewisham as 'sun-baked, mottled with lichens and topped with moss'. But that was too much for Holmes. Yet the Master continually set an example of periphrastic verbosity. When there was every need to be up and away upon the heels of villainy he would prose away to Watson like this, 'I admit to you that the case, which seemed to me so absurdly simple as to be hardly worth my notice, is rapidly assuming a very different aspect. It is true that, though in your mission you have missed everything of importance, yet even those things which have obtruded themselves upon your notice give rise to serious thought'. Suggested translation. 'I thought it was too simple a case for me, but it isn't. You missed what mattered at Lewisham, but what you did manage to see was something important.' I cannot remember whether Holmes was ever disturbed while reading Gibbon, but his conversation suggests that he might have been.

Did Doyle give Holmes this kind of fire-side style as part of a literary convention? Or did gentlemen of the 'nineties really talk like that? At any rate, Holmes rarely, if ever, described a criminal as 'getting away'; he was always 'effecting his escape'. But I deviate from cravats.

DAST

THE American language occasionally shelters its relics of old English in a strange assemblage of new slang. I was astonished to come across dast for darest in Damon Runyon's Broadway. In a restaurant, night-haunt of Regret the Horse-player (a name for a gambler almost good enough in its admonitory way for Bunyan himself) of Israel Ib, Sam the Gonoph, Lovey Lou and many another minion of the moon, dast and gotten hold their place with a glorious gallimaufrey of slang-words drawn from German, Yiddish and other components of the great linguistic melting-pot.

Runyon's racy yarns of the horse-players, the crap-shooters and their kind make me wonder why money should be called among these gentry, who were so much concerned in somehow getting hold of it, by such drab and unalluring terms as scratch and potatoes. Why a thing should be called sugar at one moment and scratch or potatoes the next I do not understand. But perhaps these words have wilted away by now. There is nothing which has such rapidly changing slang as money. Does anybody speak in Britain of oof and oof-bird today? Do schoolboys still ask each other if they have got any tin? And what of 'the ready', which was in use, I believe, in Tudor English? I surmise that sugar, with sugar-baby and sugar-daddy to signify acquisitive young women and their amorous seniors of the other sex, will probably survive on Broadway. At least sugar has the flavour of what it means, which scratch and potatoes have not.

Before we leave Runyon let us salute the word fink. In the tale of *Princess O'Hara* it is written,

> It comes out that the guy with him is really a fink by the name of Joe the Blow Fly, but he is really only a fink in every respect, a fink being such a guy as is extra nothing, and many citizens are somewhat surprised when they learn that Fats O'Rourke is going around with finks.

Again we meet finkishness in Count Tomaso of *Cemetery Bait*.

> In fact Count Tomaso claims to belong to the Italian nobility, but he is no more a Count than I am, and to tell the truth, he is nothing but a ginzo out of Sacramento and his right name is Carfarelli.

Tomaso, for twenty years 'on the socket', was a blackmailer who 'put the shakes' in 'foolish old married judys' and could 'nine those old phlugs in first-class style when he was knuckling'.

41

In fact, concludes Runyon, 'Count Tomaso is regarded in some circles as a 22-carat fink, a fink being a character who is lower than a mud-cat's vest pocket'.

I know nothing of mud-cats and their haberdashery, but plainly that settles the fink.

DEMONSTRATEE

THE Lord Chief Justice of England has protested against the use in court of this word to signify the customer to whom a possible purchase is shown. Certainly we permit mortgagee and lessee, but we do not turn a buyer into a vendee or a tutor's pupil into a tutee. We allow examinees, but we do not permit them also to be called invigilatees because their supervisor is an invigilator. Nor do mentors, so far, have mentees. It is bad enough to listen to some of our lecturing sages: worse, far worse, to be called their mentees. But I never was fond of the word mentor: it is too often the pseudonym of appallingly dull and ill-written letters in local papers, composed in reply, as a rule, to the equally ill-phrased indignation of *Fiat Justitia*. I attribute the broken pen-nibs in hotel writing-rooms to the heavy-handed epistolary zeal of Mentor and his tribe.

Reference to the dictionary informs me that a fusee is not a thing fused, but was derived from the Latin *fusus*, a spindle, and so meant originally a spindleful of tow. It is also an 'exostosis upon one of the cannon-bones'. (I look up cannon-bones: they are the single bones between the knee or hough and fetlock of a horse or other quadruped. This reminds me of a recent vogue-song, 'Dem Bones'). But I wander from demonstratee. It is dangerous to start poking about in dictionaries: there is no end to the meanderings they invite. There may be matter here for cross-word-puzzle-makers when fusee comes their way. No dictionary will allow them demonstratee, I fancy. But that may come. Even a Lord Chief Justice cannot put down verbal crime.

DEMURE

F E W words better look or sound their part than does demure.

> Come pensive Nun, devout and pure,
> Sober, steadfast, and demure,

sang Milton in *Il Penseroso*. But all were not so fond of demureness. Certainly not Falstaff.

> There's never none of these demure boys come to any proof;
> for their drink doth so over-cool their blood and the making
> many fish-meals that they fall into a kind of male green-sick-
> ness; and then, when they marry, they get wenches; they are
> generally fools and cowards; which some of us should be too,
> but for inflammation.

Demure is presumably derived from moeurs, behaviour, and fits the dimly moral person. I was brought up on the doctrine that fish builds brain, which view Falstaff's 'generally fools' strongly contradicts. It is now less confidently affirmed. If cod-consumption fathers intellect, then Britain, with the derisory meat-ration allotted to it at the time of writing, ought to be rich in demure cerebration. But I doubt whether diet greatly affects the mental operations. Beef-eaters may have brilliant wits and the feast of reason may flourish on a flow of sole.

Shakespeare used demure as a verb. His Cleopatra was not going to have Octavia demuring upon her.

DEOCHANDORUS

S I R H A R R Y L A U D E R so widely popularized this Gaelic name for the old stirrup-cup and the modern 'one for the road', that most English can now mutter 'Jock and Doris' when they imply a last glass. The *Scottish National Dictionary*, which must surely know best, gives deochandorus as the principal spelling of this door-drink. But Sir Walter Scott wrote 'Some thrust out their snuff-mulls for the parting pinch — others tendered the doch-an-dorrach' and Scots in general have spelled their parting cup in all sorts of ways, including the English-looking Doris.

> Some drouthy billies tak a tour
> Roon a' the bars o' Forres
> And bide beyond th' allotted oor
> To hae a dochan doris.

(Incidentally, what a much better word is drouthy than thirsty.)

The origin is plain enough. Deoch is Gaelic for a drink and dorus is a door. And the English music-hall, echoing a Scottish chorus, has adopted and Anglicized the Gaelic term for a final tassie.

DIMETHYLAMINOETHANOL

CHEMISTRY is now the most profuse word-spinner in the land, and has a wondrous abracadabra of its own. (The doctrine of evolution was called 'abracadabra' in 1879.) For polysyllabic mystery it rivals even the minor railway-stations and village names of Wales. I suppose this is the only way in which the niceties of chemical composition can be set on paper, but I should not care to be a student who had to get every syllable right in the nervous stress of an examination. Consider this piece of information taken from a trade paper, *The Manufacturing Chemist*.

> When ethylene oxide reacts with secondary amines such as dimethylamine and diethylamine, dialkylaminoethanols are among the products obtained. Diethylaminoethanol is an intermediate in the preparation of procaine and procaine penicillin; dimethylaminoethanol is an intermediate in the

44

preparation of some of the anti-histamine drugs. Dialkyl-laminoethanols have also been suggested as constituents in the preparation of urea-formaldehyde resins designed particularly for promoting 'wet strength' in kraft papers. Ethylene oxide itself is an excellent fumigant.

The life-saving penicillin has somewhat complicated origins, at least verbally. I am glad that they gave penicillin so simple a name. Suppose we had to supplicate our doctors for a tablet or 'shot' of Dimethylaminoethanol!

DISPLENISH

W H E N furniture and gear were to be sold up in Scotland, one saw 'Displenish' 'teckit up upon the yett' (gate). What a formal, lawyer-like announcement of domestic tragedy.

The afore-mentioned Aberdeenshire (and alcoholic) miller, made the sad process an occasion.

> Nae doot, at the Widow's displenish,
> Gey aften I emptied the stoup;
> But thrift is a thing we should cherish,
> An' whisky's aye free at a roup.

What a world in which a roup (auction-sale) involved free whisky! Our Welfare State knows none of this generosity. An old colleague of mine once told me that his first journalistic assignment, when he was a reporter in Aberdeen, was to describe the village celebration of Queen Victoria's Diamond Jubilee. On the mid-day dinner table was a half-bottle of whisky for every man, woman and child. Some fortunate parents had six or more children. Nowadays we have children's milk, children's allowances, but not rations of that kind. No bishoping, but possibly some sitting and peching on that afternoon.

DOOF

THE Scots have a most satisfying variety of words for a blow: doof comes high up in the scale of violence, as is shown by this vigorous piece of 'Lallans' in a story by James Hogg, the Ettrick Shepherd. In a tale called *The Brownie of Bodsbeck* John Hoy, a herdsman, is examined by Claverhouse about some soldiers found killed.

'How did it appear to you that they had been slain? Were they cut with swords, or pierced with bullets?'

'I canna say, but they war sair hashed.'

'How do you mean when you say they were hashed?'

'Champit like; a'broozled and jurmummled, as it were.'

'Do you mean that they were cut, or cloven, or minced?'

'Na, na, — no that ava. But they had gotten some sair doofs. They had been terribly paikit and daddit wi' something.'

'I do not in the least conceive what you mean.'

'That's extr'ord'nar', man — can ye no understand folk's mother-tongue? I'll mak it plain to ye. Ye see, whan a thing comes on ye that gate, that's a dadd — sit still now. Then a paik, that's a swap or skelp like — when a thing comes on ye that way, that's a paik. But a doof's warst ava — it's —'

'Prithee hold; I now understand it all perfectly well.'

Of these skelp is perhaps the most frequently used today. I am reminded of a night-watchman on a rickety Scottish pier that had been much neglected. When it was suggested to him that a steamer coming in with a strong side-wind and a big sea running might knock it to pieces, he remarked reflectively, 'Ay, ane guid skelp and we're awa'.' Then he settled down, unperturbed, to await what skelps might awa' with him. Happily the pier is still there, no doubt reinforced by now. But had the accident occurred on a rough day, the patient watchman and his charge would surely have been daddit, paikit, doofed, champit, broozled and jurmummled.

DROSHKY AND SHANDRYDAN

'REPAIRS to Droshky' figured in an early Victorian account-book of an East of Scotland joiner. Nowadays we use droshky as a jocose term for any antiquated horse-vehicle, but Baltic influence had made it almost a normal Scottish word for a four-wheeled carriage in the early nineteenth century. Sir Walter Scott has droshkys at large on his roads and of course there was no note of patronage in the use of the name then. Shandrydan, which I suspect was Irish in origin, was a hooded chaise which became a symbol of all rickety conveyances. The reference to 'our old shandrydan' was a modest allusion to the family vehicle, which may once have been amusing but soon ceased to be. 'Origin obscure.' But the look and sound of this species of droshky proclaims decay, collapsed springs and a wheel that may soon part company.

DRUMBLE

'LOOK how you drumble', cries Mistress Ford to the servants who are supposed to be smothering Falstaff in the linen of the washing-basket. Drumble, for to muddle in a lazy way, is an excellent word; it has something of the drone and something of tumble. It is also a noun, meaning a loutish idler. The errand-boy is now a rarity; he can find higher employment, which is doubtless well for him, though not so well for the house-wife who has to do all her own collecting and cartage. At one time he was often a notable example of the drumble, swift to drop but slow to pick up, a great whistler of the tune of the day, no scorcher of the pavement as he trod his way, basket on arm. Slow trains drumble too, as they groan in the sun beside the sleepy canal from Abbots' Pottering to Compton Baskerville and similar abodes of sloom. (*See* Sloomy later.) There are times when it is pleasant to be a drumble in a drumbling train and to watch the heat-hazed inertia of a July afternoon. Drumbling trains are only infuriating when they are supposed to be racing expresses, on whose punctuality you have put reliance. London has its drumble buses, those which have got ahead of their time-schedule and now purposely lag so as to miss every traffic-light and thus avoid, by dawdling, the sin of being previous. Since sitting in a London bus, with some engagement to keep, is rarely a blissful session, such drumbles cause bad temper. But if you were to echo Mistress Ford and say to the conductor 'Look, how you drumble', there is little chance of your Shakespearean lore being appreciated.

DUNGEON

'Before Dr. Johnson came to breakfast,' said Lady Lochbuy, 'he was a dungeon of wit', a very common phrase to express a profoundness of intellect.' Thus Boswell. It is certainly a gloomy metaphor to use, but it may suit the more macabre or misanthropic type of Scottish sage. Lady Lochbuy (we would spell it Lochbuie) then offered the Doctor cold sheep's head for his breakfast, which her brother, Sir Allan, regarded as 'vulgarity'. Johnson was surprised and angry, says Boswell, at this bleak aspect of Hebridean morning hospitality. But, when you have likened a man to a dungeon, cold mutton for breakfast may seem a natural offer.

Dungeon, originating from the Latin *dominus* and meaning instrument of dominion and domination, is a properly awesome word. When Othello said that before he shared his love he would

rather be a toad
And live upon the vapour of a dungeon.

he drove into the bottom depths of squalor. No, for a man of high intelligence — for this Lady Lochbuy surely meant in her use of the word wit — to be likened to a fetid subterranean cell is hard. There is no evidence that Dr. Johnson liked the phrase any more than he liked cold sheep's head for breakfast, an offer to which he said 'no, madam', without even a 'thank you'.

DYNAMITARD

A *Times* Fourth leader protests against the existence and usage of Dynamitard. Yet, according to *O.E.D.*, the composer of this pleasant piece is being sniffy about the habits of his own profession. For Oxford lexicography says coldly of this imposing alternative to dynamiter ['Newspapers']. The square brackets are uncommonly like cold shoulders and the tone of the observation reminds one rather of a seeker for lodgings who, sniffing the atmosphere of the offered shelter, mutters disconsolately, 'mice'.

Yet the termination -ard to suggest a doer of this or that is elsewhere tolerated. Drinkers who exceed are permitted to be drunkards and the practitioners of sluggishness are allowed to be sluggards. Indeed, the same volume of collected 'Fourths' contains a note entitled 'The Happy Sluggard'. Of old a bumble-bee could be a bumbard because of his active bumbling and a bombard was an early contrivance for hurling explosive. Merely to touch off dynamite now seems, in a world of far more drastic detonations, a minor form of violence, but I remember reading with awe about anarchistic dynamitards. They sounded more terrible than mere dynamiters. Where, by the way, is the accent in dynamitard? On the 'am' or on a long 'y'? Seeking analytical knowledge, I find that dynamite is a preparation of nitro-glycerine 'mixed for safety with some inert absorptive substance'. But there was no safety or inertia when dynamitards were at work. 'Inert absorptive substance' is charming and happily describes the frame of a somnolent but just conscious listener to the droning of a dull sermon.

EAGER

T o be eager is now to be keen; to call a man eager is hardly to impute a vice. Yet eager was originally sour: it is our form of aigre. Chaucer used it of sharp medicine. In Daniel George's rich scrapbook called *Now and Then* I read of a 'Hackett, William, a fam'd Imposter', who later 'played the Hypocrite, counterfeited Sanctity, was taken by some deluded weak People to be the Messiah, and was later hanged at Tyburn for Blasphemy and Treason. In his childhood at Oundle he was so Cruel, Eager, and Insolent that he bit off his Schoolmaster's Nose and eat it before his Face, as he pretended to embrace him out of Love'.

At Oundle nowadays, where, I trust, the Lesser Cannibalism is no longer practised by the eager young at the expense of the ushers and their nebs, eat in this passage would be spelled ate. But one often finds eat as a past tense in the classics. Eager has come up in the world, as Master Hackett went steadily down from form-room to gibbet.

ESEMPLASTIC

WE live in the Age of Plastics, but I see no reason for encouraging the survival of this one. Coleridge used it of the imagination, but the Higher Criticism, in its efforts to seem erudite, surely need not drag it in. Some dictionaries ignore the Grecian quadrisyllable; it means no more than moulding or unifying. 'Criticese' can be a dreadful jargon, written to impress, not to illumine. When in one of the loftier journals I find reference to the esemplastic powers of an author's mind, I am both deterred from reading the author, which may be unfair, and wearied by the assessor who cannot say mould or unify when he means it. Puddering about with such verbal plasticene is a game for grown-up babies. Shakespeare, when writing of the poet's fancy, managed well enough without ransacking the lexicon for esemplastic. His pedantic Holofernes might have invented it, but that job was left to Coleridge whose poetic genius is not diminished if we say that his prose was occasionally guilty of 'criticese'.

FABULOUS

F A B U L O U S, at the time of my writing, is the pet-word of English journalism, and the particular joy of the colourful reporter. Everything at all large or in the least strange is described as fabulous. In one popular paper I have today seen it applied both to an actress and to a huge industrial company, to the first because of her unique appeal, to the second because of its millions of capital.

The real meaning of fabulous, as applied to persons, is fond of recounting fables or of listening to fables. Of things or monsters it means mythical or legendary. It is therefore a debatable point whether the Loch Ness Monster which appears, or is believed to appear, from time to time on the surface of the long, dark, deep waters of the Great Glen of the Scottish Highlands, is fabulous or not. The nonsense begins when footballers are described as fabulous because they are efficient, industrial enterprises because they are highly capitalized and film-stars because they have Oomph, It, or whatever is the current word for sexual magnetism.

Old wives, incidentally, are supposed to be fabulous in the correct sense, fond of hearing or repeating fables. How many could say offhand where the phrase 'Old Wives' fables' first appears? St. Paul, in his First Epistle to Timothy, exhorted his correspondent thus, 'But refuse profane and old wives' fables and exercise thyself rather unto godliness', presumably referring to improper stories and silly lies. Shakespeare used fabulous simply to mean false. Modern journalism employs it to mean wonderful, but true; for surely modern journalism, when writing of fabulous folk and things, is not indulging in falsehoods but merely giving colour to truth. At least, as a journalist, I hope so for the honour of my craft; but not very confidently. Some sections of the Press, seeking, in the new sense, fabulous sales may become fabulous in the old and proper meaning, as they do so.

FANTOOSH

T H I S is cheating, because it is not an English word or even common Scots. But the Scottish lexicographers admit it as a fairly recent term for flashily fashionable. As such, it is magnificent. The implied mixture of fancy or fantasy and tosh so nicely sums up the uniforms of spivery. I have never possessed one of the more pictorial neckties favoured by the barrow-boy who has also ambitions to be a buck, bean or blade. But, if I did enscarf myself so, I should be happy to be called fantoosh.

FIEND

A F I E N D was originally any hated one, any enemy, any opposite to friend. (From old English, feon, to hate.) But, when enemy became a general term of common use, the fiend was particularized as the enemy of the soul, the Hated One of all good Christians, the Devil. Though Shakespeare and Milton used it freely and powerfully of things Satanic, it is an odd fact, as Henry Bradley pointed out in *The Making of English*, that there is no Fiend mentioned in the Bible or the Prayer-Book. Yet Bunyan used it of his Apollyon.

Shakespeare's texts, from *Titus Andronicus* onwards, screech of fiends, in fearsome plenty, often with the adjective foul or with the suffix 'of hell'. The implication was still that a fiendish fellow is a man Satanically possessed: the adjective fiendish, which has now, like devilish, been weakened to mean little more than nasty (e.g. 'fiendish weather we're having') is not in Shakespeare at all. It was an odd fancy of Blake's that he put in 'Infant Sorrow',

> My mother groan'd, my father wept,
> Into the dangerous world I leapt;
> Helpless, naked, piping loud
> Like a fiend hid in a cloud.

If fiend has been degraded in the current employment both of the noun and of the adjective fiendish, the Scots have played down this form of devil even further. Their word 'fient' now means little more than scarcely. 'Fient a chiel was there' suggests scarcely anybody present. The English might also say 'Devil a man to be seen'. But they would not say 'Fiend a fellow about'. The Scots, turning fiend to fient, would do so. They have reduced the foul fiend Flibbertigibbet, 'who squints the eye and makes the hare-lip, mildews the white wheat and hurts the poor creatures of the earth' — a Fiend indeed — to be the faint shadow of a mild expletive. What a fall for Lucifer! Mention of the Fiend and his devilish tricks brings to mind a superb remark made to me by a London bus-conductor. We were going along Oxford Street on a Saturday night and passed an enthusiastic young man who was walking along in the road brandishing a banner announcing the love of Jesus. He raucously called us all to salvation through a megaphone. The conductor looked with tolerant amusement at this emissary of heaven and said, 'He does it for devilment'.

FINNIMBRUNS

READERS of *The Compleat Angler* will encounter Finnimbruns, but I am not aware that they will meet this finery anywhere else. *O.E.D.* cites no other example. Finnimbruns were the trinkets and fal-lals likely to be bought at old-time fairs. They were the stock-in-trade of Autolycus, 'riband, glass, pomander, brooch, table-book, ballad, knife, tape, glove, shoe-tie, bracelet, horn-ring', and

> Gloves as sweet as damask-roses,
> Masks for faces and for noses;
> Bugle-bracelet, necklace-amber,
> Perfume for a lady's chamber;

> Golden quoifs and stomachers
> For my lads to give their dears;
> Pins and poking-sticks of steel,
> What maids lack from head to heel.

Autolycus had a fair-sized cargo of finnimbruns and, though he talks of his pack and is usually staged with no more than that amount of small baggage, he really should arrive with a go-cart if he is to include

> lawn as white as driven snow

Quoif and stomachers (caps and 'ornamental coverings for the breast and upper abdomen'), if carried in profitable quantity, would alone occupy considerable space in any pack of finnimbruns.

How did this word happen? Plainly it began with finery; but of what are the 'imbruns' a corruption? The dictionary cites, as a parallel to this word, the coninbrum which a conundrum occasionally became; the origin of conundrum is itself a conundrum; it is probably a mixture of some Latin words. Imbrue meant to dye or stain before it was specially applied to blood (e.g. Ancient Pistol's 'shall we imbrue?') So finnimbruns might possibly be a slurred form of fine imbruings, i.e. of fine coloured stuffs and bright gew-gaws.

FLOWER-DE-LUCE

IT is odd how lines and half-lines of poetry vibrate in the memory for no particular reason. They may do so for reasons more of oddity than of beauty. At one time the list of near-Eastern potentates and 'kings o' the earth' assembled for war by Shakespeare's Antony used to rumble in my sub-conscious. 'Bocchus the king of Libya' and 'King Malchus of Arabia; King of Pont' came unbidden to my lips, especially Bocchus who so delightfully sounds like a mixture of the wine-god and Sir Toby Belch. On another plane, 'The flower-de-luce being one' has been a haunting half-line. Why?

> Lilies of all kinds,
>   The flower-de-luce being one

is almost catalogue English. In poetic value it is not nearly as fair of phrase as the preceding tribute to the March-daring daffodils and the pale primroses

> That die unmarried, ere they can behold
> Bright Phoebus in his strength.

Yet the flower-de-luce lurks no less happily within me.

The Tudor variant on fleur-de-lys was specially applied to the Iris. Spencer's

> The lilly, lady of the flowring field,
> The flowre-deluce her lovely paramoure

is richer far than Shakespeare's curt and austere lily-register, 'The flower-de-luce being one'. The royal emblem of France and the symbol of its chivalry wields no less fascination when it nods so simply on an English river-bank.

The Scottish variant, segg, is certainly no charmer to the ear. Yet, in Charles Murray's Aberdeenshire of the *Hamewith* poems, it blooms with beauty, despite the gruff monosyllable. In 'Spring in the Howe o' Alford' the seggs are dew-bright.

> The liftward lark lea's the dewy seggs,
> In the hedge the yeldrin's singin';
> The teuchat cries for her harried eggs,
> In the bothy window hingin'.

Liftward, for the benefit of the English-Speaking Union, is sky-ward. (The modern writers of 'Lallans' make the sky usually luft, not lift.) If segg is no rival in sound to flower-de-luce, yeldrin can claim to improve on yellow-hammer.

FUSTIAN

CLOTH-NAMES are nearly always place-names. I was surprised to find that Fustian, 'a thick, twilled cloth with a short pile or nap now usually dyed a dark colour' is an Egyptian. Its home was Fostat, a suburb of Cairo. I cannot say why such a plain textile should have given a title to pretentious, high flown talk and drunken babblings. 'Drunk? And speak parrot? And squabble? Swagger? Swear? And discourse fustian with one's own shadow.' Thus Cassio. Yet Shakespeare also used fustian to mean serviceable cloth, 'serving-men in their new fustian'. The meaning of rant has clung, most oddly, to this dull and economical material which was never showy and never carried any visual rhetoric.

> And he whose fustian's so sublimely bad
> It is not poetry, but prose run mad

occurs in Pope's Epistle to Dr. Arbuthnot, although fustian as a cloth was modesty itself, the servitor's symbol.

Having its origin in Fostat, fustian has no connection with our other 'fusty' words: they are a rich collection including fustigate, for cudgel, and fustilugs, a gross, lumpy person or corpulent woman. Fustilugs is not a term which should be left to 'fust in us unused'. Gross louts are well served in English. I liked especially a looby, but let us remember fustilugs among the rest. Fustian has had one picturesque child, fustanella, the white cotton kilt worn by men in modern Greece.

GALLOW

IS gallow, to frighten, derived from the terror associated with the gallows? The dictionary looks back to an old English word meaning alarm, which created the verb to gally for to scare. ('Now dialect and in the whale fishery'.) I cannot see why this gally should have fathered the gallow used by Kent in the Storm Scene in *King Lear*.

> The wrathful skies
> Gallow the very wanderers of the dark
> And make them keep their caves.

Why should the shorter gally make the longer gallow? I suspect that the fear inspired by the gibbet and its burden of flesh — a fairly common spectacle in Tudor times — was the source of gallow as a transitive verb. Scare-crow has been gally-crow in its time and there again the fantastic and fearsome figure in the field might plainly be derived from the gibbeted corpse.

The hangman's gallows began as 'a gallow', but the plural prevailed. Was the word ever better used with sinister suggestion than in Gonzalo's remark concerning the Boatswain in *The Tempest*, 'His complexion is perfect gallows!' That suits so well the waxy pallor of those gallow-birds who stand in the Chamber of Horrors at Madame Tussaud's.

Then the double plural gallowses came into the vernacular. Said the humane First Gaoler in *Cymbeline* 'O there were desolation of gaolers and gallowses! I speak against my present profit'. From these gallowses, the merciless suspenders of a corpse, came descent to the blameless utility of the haberdashers' suspenders and braces. Gallus or galluses is, I suppose, dismissable as dialect. But it is still commonly used in certain parts of the country to signify the safeguard of the trousered man.

GENTEEL

GENTLE came from the Latin gens and referred to high birth and high birth in the age of chivalry meant courtesy and humility. The gentle man was both well-born and well-mannered.

Genteel is only gentle with another spelling, but now it implies a sneer. Yet when Pepys described a dinner as the 'genteelest' he had come across, he was paying a gracious compliment to style of service and amenity of menu. Lord Chesterfield asked his son, 'Have you learned to carve? Do you use yourself to carve adroitly or genteelly, without hacking half an hour across a bone, without bespattering the company with the sauce, and without overturning the glasses into your neighbours pockets?' To be genteel with the knife was to avoid violence and to display efficiency. 'Most vices', said Doctor Johnson, 'may be committed very genteelly: a man may debauch his friend's wife very genteelly; he may cheat at cards genteelly.' The doctor was not demeaning 'genteelity' when he spoke thus. Or has a faint sneer begun?

The nineteenth century strengthened, if it did not introduce, the note of derision. The genteel man was the gentleman fussily self-conscious of his quality and refusing to admit decline of status. So came the dismissal of those clinging amid their poverty to the dignities of class as 'shabby genteel'. (There is surely a heroism about shabby gentility which the dismissive phrase obscures.) 'Dialect words — those terrible marks of the beast to the truly genteel.' When Thomas Hardy wrote that he was denouncing linguistic snobbishness with a term that had lost its old honour. The 'truly genteel' man has sunk to the level of a pretender.

Genteel is an adaptation of the French gentil. While gentle retained its complimentary meaning (as genteel did for several centuries) the -eel termination began to seem comic and to invite a playful sarcasm. I suppose there are other words whose separate pronunciations have different meanings? But I cannot immediately think of them.

Some early verses, by Robert Burns, those on 'handsome Nell' Kilpatrick, used genteel without derision.

> She dresses aye sae clean and neat.
>   Baith decent and genteel.
> And then there's something in her gait
>   Gars ony dress look weel.

They are scarcely inspired, but I am sure that Nell took no offence at 'decent and genteel'.

GOOSE

THE common theatrical phrase 'Get the Bird' must come, I suppose, from the noise of hissing; and an angry goose hisses. There is thus the implication, consoling for the victim of 'a bird', that the audience are geese not to appreciate his points. Nowadays one hears it said that 'so and so got a screaming bird'. But this kind of reception is wrongly so named. It was once a hiss; it is now as a rule, not a scream but a melancholy moan.

At any rate to goose was Victorian English for hiss in the showman's world. When poor Jupe, in *Hard Times*, was doing feebly in Sleary's Circus-ring Mr. E. W. B. Childers, 'so justly famous for his daring vaulting act as the Wild Huntsman of the North American Prairies', said of the poor wretch, 'He was goosed last night, he was goosed the night before, he was goosed today. He has lately got into the way of being always goosed. And he can't stand it.'

Mr. Gradgrind inquired about this Goosing, 'forcing the word out of himself with great solemnity and reluctance'. Mr. Childers replied that poor Jupe's limbs were turning stiff, but that he had still had points as a Cackler, i.e. talker. Jupe had been 'missing his tips' and loose in his ponging (short in his leaps and bad in his tumbling). Hence the goose-hiss and the bitter chagrin of Jupe. 'It cut that man deeper', concluded E. W. B. Childers 'to know that his daughter knew of his being goosed than to go through with it.'

I never hear this verb of menace used today. But as a firstnighter I hear, on dismal occasions, the groan from aloft which has taken its place. It resembles no utterance of any bird, save possibly, the last of the owl's four syllables. But 'get the bird' seems to be well fixed now as a description of this misery.

GRENADIER

Evelyn's Diary mentions 'a new sort of soldiers called Grenadiers who are dexterous in flinging hand grenades'. But the grenado or grenade, which was also a pomegranate, was known before Evelyn alluded to it. Donne used it in a poem on what the publicists of romantic films and stories call 'flaming desire'.

> Woe to her stubborn heart, if once mine come
> Into the self-same room,
> T'will tear and blow up all within,
> Like a grenado shot into a magazin.

Grenades are not usually 'shot'. But let that pass. I like to think of Miss Grable described as a blonde grenado.

A kindlier species of grenado was 'A dish of larded veal-collops, with six pigeons and a ragout in the middle, covered above and below with thin slices of bacon'. Who would not be a grenadier in this cause? For the Britain of 1951, simultaneously confronted with rearmament and fed with a 'match-box' meat-ration, one kind of grenado has its utility, the other has a far-off fascination.

HA-HA

From time to time one is reminded by the more informative type of journalism that there is a Ha-Ha Road in the Woolwich area. I have seen it stated that this thoroughfare does not resound with residential laughter because there are no houses in it. There should be no houses in a Ha-Ha, since the article is a sunken and hidden road which makes a boundary. It properly surrounded elegant pleasure-grounds whose occupants wished to be private and yet not to be deprived of their view by anything so vulgarly or unhandsomely upstanding as a fence. So the separation from the outer world was achieved by a track in a trench, which presumably surprised those who came upon it suddenly and evoked the exclamation, Ha, ha.

I came across ha-ha in connection with the French guingette. Atticus of *The Sunday Times* lamented the fact that the Prince Regent never built the ha-ha-girt guingette in the middle of Regent's Park as he intended: Atticus called in John Summerson's book on Nash to identify a guingette: it is 'a pleasure resort outside the jurisdiction of municipal housing authorities' and the use of the term suggested that 'the prince's intentions were of a holiday nature'. A guingette would obviously be obnoxious to a Planned Economy or Paradise of Puffingtons. But it sounds, especially when complete with ha-ha, a cordial, seductive spot.

HONG AND MIDOR

TRANSPORT workers' English is a subject that has considerable curiosities. I have explained elsewhere how, in my boyhood, the London tubes had door-shutting attendants on the coaches; their task was to announce to supposedly comatose or ignorant passengers what the next stop would be. At Goodge Street it was their habit to roar Torracorranex, which meant that the Tottenham Court Road station was adjacent. So the thoroughfare has always remained Torracorra to me.

Nowadays there are no such proclamations of proximity. But there are men and women in uniform who appear on the platforms at the rush hours in much-frequented stations to bellow or scream Hong and Midor. Hong is apparently their version of Hurry Along and Midor means Mind the Doors. Their uproar is the more vexatious since everybody is 'honging' as hard as he or she can and to be scolded as a dilatory slacker when one is desperately striving to be somehow wedged into the carriage is, to me at least, maddening. Moreover the Midor yell is no less exasperating since it is impossible to mind anything, be it manners, doors, or the corns on one's feet, when one is simply a unit in a swirling and congealed mass and so utterly incapable of any individual choice of motion.

None the less, hong strikes me as a useful word. To describe a person as honging to it does suggest a desperate endeavour to keep up with a stampede, half hurrying, half just hanging on. Midor, on the other hand is so obviously a mixture of Midas and his gold that it should be the name given one day to an all-conquering race-horse.

It must be very difficult for foreign visitors, with Hong and Midor ringing in their ears, to have any notion of what is intended. Moreover, when they leave London, they must find our British accents so widely dissimilar that the remarks of railway workers will be mostly incomprehensible. Though a Scot and capable of dealing with most Scottish speech, I have the greatest trouble in interpreting the language used by the staff in Glasgow railway-stations, where the words are not so much spoken as gargled very deep in the throat. Perhaps few strangers wish to invade that district of Glasgow so handsomely called Strathbungo, but, if they did, would they ever recognize its vocally condensed form?

IMMOTE

RUPERT BROOKE used the rare immote for motionless in his 'Dining-Room Tea', but I do not think that he did so in affectation. It was the similarity of sound and lettering with immortal that suggested it and the result justifies the archaism.

> For suddenly and other whence
> I looked on your magnificence.
> I saw the stillness and the light
> And you august, immortal, white,
> Holy and strange: and every glint
> Posture and jest and thought and tint
> Freed from the mask of transiency,
> Triumphant in eternity,
> Immote, immortal.

As a pattern of internal and external alliteration, possibly subconscious, this passage is worth notice. T is the dominant letter, but the ms are subtly interlaced. The repetition of immortal may be care — or carelessness. I surmise the former. The first immortal sets the tune for the two grave, sonorous adjectives of the close. Immote is a splendidly picturesque word and states a restful permanence with solid power. Motionless and immobile seem feeble beside it.

IMPECCABLE

IMPECCABLE properly means 'not liable to sin'. To his Church the Pope is both impeccable and infallible. The adjective has now become a favourite with critics when in kindly mood. 'An impeccable performance.' Since it is a common habit of those who write advertisement copy to apply to articles the epithets natural to persons ('This courteous sleeping-suit', 'These humane slippers', 'This good-tempered purge') impeccable is an obvious acquisition. I have just been invited to buy 'an impeccable rain-coat with implicit style'. Well, the coat may begin as a model of seemly virtue, but in my own case rain-coats soon begin to 'pecc' and, instead of retaining their implicit style, they develop explicit droops and bulges. The fault is, no doubt, my own. I was not shaped for haberdashers' joy.

Mention of Advertisers' English has brought me the reminder that Slenderize is now a verb of common use and that 'Tenderized Prunes' are on the market. They must be 'impeccably processed' to achieve this delicacy beyond prunish nature. The same correspondent informs me that some London milk-carts bear the baffling but appealing inscription, 'Designated Milk', derived, I presumed, from impeccable cows with implicit hygiene.

Advertisers, when they are not being pseudo-scientific, are the poets of our time. I constantly admire the ingenuity with which the Counsel for Salesmanship manages to screw a new adjective or metaphor from our hard-worked language. Surely 'whisper-light' is a charming adjective for a silk — I have just come across it in *Vogue* — and much better than 'bubble-dainty' applied to a similar fabric. Who can resist shoes 'interpreted in glove-soft suède'. Interpreted is a fine invention; here is the shoe-maker as impeccable translator of implicit style.

INCOME

An income in Scotland, and the North of England, is, or was, an ailment of unknown source. During the 1914-18 war medical casualties were often labelled P.U.O., which meant Pyrexia of Uncertain Origin, in fact Income. This saved the doctors a deal of trouble in more exact diagnosis and many Scottish medicos may have muttered 'Its an Income' to cover their inability to be more precise. Thus their other kind of income was easily earned.

In English the word income was originally a spiritual inflow, an entry of grace. (In much the same way the odious influenza is descended from Influence, which was specially applied to 'the supposed flowing from the stars of an etheral fluid acting upon the character and destiny of men and affecting sublunary things generally'.) While influence has sunk to be a pyrexia, income has fallen from heavenly virtue and inspiration to be the prop of man's power to survive in a commercial society. 'The pure Incomes of a Holy Life' have become the earned or unearned cash in hand or in the bank. Income has also been an entrance fee or gate money. Since we have an Entertainment Duty, your income to the pictures raids your own income to increase the income of the State. Nowadays the frequent suffix of Income is Tax and this impost has become so damnably oppressive that it justly shares its name with a disease.

INTARISSABLE

A YOUNG writer on the theatre, Mr. Ken Tynan, makes use of intarissable. He has taken a degree in English Literature and, as I gather from his rich vocabulary and ample quotations, has been well grounded in John Donne and Sir Thomas Browne. I take it that he derived his formidable adjective, meaning not to be dried up, inexhaustible, from one of these sources. No doubt he did. But the *O.E.D.* does not cite them. It does, however, cite a Mrs. Schimmel-Penninck who, in a play called *Prince Beauty* (1859), wrote of an 'intarissable fountain of gushing joy'. Compton Mackenzie, that happily intarissable author, might have used intarissable in his earlier and magniloquent prose, along with the irremeables and other classic polysyllables. The French commonly apply the epithet to springs and wells of water, but it is rare in English.

JERK AND JERQUE

OUR English jerk has a curious assortment of meanings. It can be a stroke with the cane or whip. So Shakespeare knew it. John Brinsley, author of *Lundus Literarius* or The Grammar Schoole (1612), was a sour disciplinarian who believed that the boy was a natural vessel of Original Sin, which could be 'jerked' out of him by the rod.

> But herein there must be special care that, when boys are restrained from play, either usher or master, if it can be conveniently, have an eye to them that they cannot loiter; or someone specially appointed, to see that they do their tasks. Also that they be called to an account the next morning whether they have done the tasks enjoined, under pain of six jerks to be surely paid.

The odious Brinsley, a sanctimonious flagellant, added this on the subject of jerking.

The rod is God's instrument. To spare them in these cases is to hate them. To love them is to correct them betime. Do it under God and for Him to these ends and with these cautions and you shall never hate them: you have the Lord for your warrant.

From jerks of this kind came the use of jerk as a stinging remark or smart, witty saying; the contemporary use of wise-crack and its shorter form crack have the same suggestion of a whip's noise. To jerk, as a verb, was to carp, nag, or gird. Shrews had jerking tongues. Jerk has survived mainly as a word for quick movement. It was already that for Shakespeare's Holofernes, who spoke of the 'jerks of invention' as one of the qualities of the poet Ovid. Or did he think of the whip-cracks of fancy? Then there is another verb jerk which means to cure meat by drying it in the sun. But this is of American Spanish origin.

Stranger still is the survival of the Norman Jerque, meaning to clear a ship. This from a Customs official:

In my branch of the Civil Service, the Customs, we are singularly free of the curse of officialese. Maybe sea breezes blow away the rubbish. But we have some fine traditional phrases (in England we are the oldest Civil Service body) and altogether merit the title once given to us at a public dinner by a pilot: 'The second oldest profession.'

We do not 'clear' a ship; we 'jerque' it (Norman English). For what the police call 'keeping observation' on a person or place we say 'staggering'. And we have a curious call when on rummage (fossick?) duties: oo ay, to hail one another or to call a ship.

The *O.E.D.* says of jerque, 'Referred to Italian *cercare* to search, but evidence is wanted'. The jerquer (the word is as old as Pepys) searched a vessel for unentered goods to see whether the cargo-list supplied by the captain agreed with the discoveries of the Customs officer. We are still subject to such jerquers when we cross the Channel, but the penalty for failure to disclose is now more financial than physical; there may have been some corporal 'jerking' of offenders in the old days, but this does not imply that jerk and jerque have the same origin.

KIOSK

T H E Chairman of the Horsham Rural Council suggested that a substitute term should be found for Kiosk. 'We don't want Russian words in our language', he said. During the battle of Stalingrad Sussex might have been 'kiosked' from Horsham to Hastings with none protesting and many applauding. But things have changed.

As a matter of fact the anti-Stalinite kioskophobes of the Weald were barking at the wrong country. The kiosk is not a Tsarist or a Marxian contraption. It is a Turkish or Persian pavilion and is mentioned by Samuel Purchas in *Purchas His Pilgrimes,* a Jacobean travel book. Kiosks have dwindled sadly: to Purchas they signified banqueting amid trellised splendours with fair views. Now they are usually mere shelters for the sale of sweets, cigarettes and newspapers. They are rarely beautiful and enthusiasts for the preservation of rural amenities are vigilant to keep them few and if possible, graciously simple. But the practice of kiosk-control need not be linked with deep political suspicions. These circular shanties are Middle Eastern but not Muscovite. The schoolboy's definition of chiaroscuro as the art of building kiosks was not much further from the truth than the notion that we stimulate Communism by getting our journals or our 'gaspers' from an English kiosk.

LAD-LASS

W E have many words for effeminacy in males from the classical epicene to the modern cissy, now replaced by pansy, queen, or pouffe. But what simpler and more direct than the Yorkshire lad-lass, applied, I think, without any vicious imputation, to one who dodges rough games and is generally weak or nervous? Yorkshire has an excellent habit of putting the old short words together. The same correspondent who gave me lad-lass, added Love-bat for 'a light, playful blow usually given to a person of the opposite sex'. Our sexual psychologists would translate this into a mild demonstration of sadistic eroticism. But love-bats will do for me. He also mentions a try-bit for sample. Sample is now, in the more solemn trade circles, called a prototype. Samples and prototypes are not really the same things, but pompous salesmen do call their samples prototypes. 'Pilot experiment' is another ambitious variant on prototype.

Try-bits are especially applied to food. One who did not like his try-bit at table, and responded with a heave of the stomach, was said to gip at it. 'If you can't eat it, leave it; don't gip at it.' A lad-lass would doubtless gip at a try-bit of boxing which involved more considerable assault than the tender love-bat.

LADY

LISTENING to one of our multitudinous Quiz programmes on the air, I found myself, as well as the learned participants, asked to say what a lady might be in professional or craft usage. She (or it) is the smallest size of Welsh and Cornish roofing-slate. Larger sizes take rank in this protocol as Countesses and Duchesses. Confirming this in the dictionary I further learned that a lady is also 'The calcareous structure in the stomach of a lobster, serving for the trituration of its food; fancifully supposed to resemble the outline of a seated female figure'. A pleasant fancy, and a most serviceable lady, since the lobster's dietary, after due gastric trituration, is transformed into such admirable flesh. (To triturate is to rub or grind down to a fine powder.) This kind lady, by the way, has to form some grisly functions of metabolism, since

I am told that, if we knew what lobsters ate, we should certainly not eat them. But I do not propose to seek that knowledge; there are often disadvantages in excess of learning.

The learned etymologists, by the way, give a queer origin to our lords and ladies — simple but superb words that have served our poets nobly. The lord, it appears, is a telescoped form of loaf-ward, the gentleman who owns and watches the bread which his scullions are to eat. The lady is said to be derived from loaf-dough; she is the kneader of the bread. Gentlemen, it is true, have often been loafers, but I am shocked to think of her ladyship as starting in menial handiwork among the dough. *O.E.D.* admits that this explanation of ladies is 'not very plausible with regard to sense' and I agree. But these appear to be the still ruling explanations of the gracious lord and his fine lady.

To loaf, for to idle or dawdle, is awarded an 'obscure origin'. Those who accept 'the conjecture (adopted in recent dictionaries) that the verb comes from German dialect lofen = laughen, to run' are put down sharply by *O.E.D.* And rightly. Running is no idle matter. So there, as they say, the matter rests in decent obscurity. To be frank, I am not strongly convinced about the loaf-ward and his loaf-dough. It is certainly odd that the terms so beautifully applied to Divine Persons should have had this larder-and-kitchen start in life. But there appears to be no alternative reason for their origin and upward climb.

Lords and ladies, having risen thus high, have also passed into botany.

> Oft under trees we nestled in a ring
> Culling out lords and ladies

sang John Clare. He was referring to *Arum Maculatum*, 'given in reference to the dark and light spadices, the dark being the lords and the light the ladies'. This reverses the colour-scheme of Shakespeare's two loves of comfort and despair. For his lord was fair and his lady very dark indeed.

LIBRARY

L A M B ridiculed the books which 'no gentleman's library can be without'. Yet there is something to be said for stateliness in folio and for the classics in calf. Libraries have come down in the world; the usual stage-set named 'the library' is a dismal matter with a travesty of book-shelves and is frequently introduced merely to be the scene of a murder. Book-shelves and blunt instruments, lethal, go together in the murder-mystery mind, which cannot think of old morocco without a millionaire 'kiboshed' and on the carpet.

More dignity was accorded to the room of books by Prospero, whose library was dukedom enough for him. In which play do the lines

> Come and take choice of all my library
> And so beguile thy sorrow —

occur? Not many will set this melodious tribute to the balm of books in its actual context. The words occur in *Titus Andronicus*, Act IV, Scene 1. Once more, library and slaughter go together.

Libraries have been put to astonishing uses. Why are the offices where people can buy theatre-tickets in London, without going to the box-office of the theatre itself, called libraries? The library at a sea-side resort a hundred years ago was obviously not visited only by the book-worms. Here is what Dickens wrote of the goings-on at one of them.

> The library was crowded. There were the same ladies, and the same gentlemen, who had been on the sands in the morning, and on the pier the day before. There were young ladies, in maroon-coloured gowns and black velvet bracelets, dispensing fancy articles in the shop, and presiding over games of chance in the concert-room. There were marriageable daughters, and marriage-making mammas, gaming and promenading, and turning over music, and flirting. There were some male

beaux doing the sentimental in whispers, and others doing the ferocious in moustaches.

They also threw dice, for reasons and reward unspecified, and they listened to professional baritones and sopranos. It was a very gay 'gentleman's library'. I am sorry to say that Sherlock Holmes spoke of a library as a mere depository. 'A man should keep his little brain attic stocked with all the furniture he is likely to use and the rest he can put away in the lumber-room of the library, where he can get it when he wants it.' That, from *The Five Orange Pips*, is deplorable doctrine, but here again crime and libraries are found together. I prefer Prospero's faith that libraries are dukedoms of the mind, not cloak-rooms or slaughter-houses.

LITH

I HAVE always been accustomed to talk about the pig of an orange to describe one of its sections. I cannot explain why. A pig, short for piggin, can be a pot or vessel. Was pig a corruption of pick, since you pick the sections out? I was reminded of this by reading in James Bridie's autobiography called *One Way of Living*, about the lith of an orange. He was describing a soldiers' improvised cocktail called a Tangerine Sling. The only available liquors were claret and rum. There were also tangerines and raisins. One tablespoonful of rum went to two of claret; the raisins were crushed into the rum and 'the juice of a single lith of orange' went into the claret. The recipe does not suggest the perfect apéritif. But 'it imparted a pleasant and enlivening sensation to the fingers and toes and made me wish to join the Flying Corps'. Lith is also a verb meaning to separate the joints one from another. Presumably one may lith a duck or a chicken and, less easily, a boiling fowl that has rashly been roasted. But are the legs and wings of poultry and game ever called liths? Boswell's father said of Cromwell, 'He gart kings ken they had a lith in their necks'.

LUMP

I WAS wondering about the phrase 'If you don't like it, you must lump it'. Lump sounds there as though it meant 'throw aside'. But it is not that. To lump is to look sulkily at, to glower, a collision, as it were of look and grumpy. There are many kinds of lumping. On the river-side, at least in Dickens's time, it was used of stealing, as well as of unloading. In his descriptive sketch *Down with the Tide*, he lists four kinds of water-thief, known to the river-police. There were Tier-rangers who silently dropped alongside the tiers of shipping in the Thames, boarded a vessel, waited for the sound of snoring and then 'groped for the skipper's inexpressibles, which it was the custom of these gentlemen to shake off, watch, money, braces and boots, all together on the floor'. It is strange to find Dickens observing the absurd Victorian convention that trousers must be disguised as unmentionables, inexpressibles or inexplicables. The next grade of robbers, the Lumpers, 'wore loose canvas jackets with a broad hem in the bottom, turned inside, so as to make a large circular pocket in which they could conceal, like clowns in pantomimes, packages of surprising size ... They also smuggled tobacco, using hydraulic presses to squeeze a single pound into a package small enough to be contained in an ordinary pocket'. After the Lumpers came Truckers, also smugglers, and Dredgemen who threw stuff overboard and dredged it up later.

To lumper has also been used as a verb, but not for thieving. It is to move lumpily and clumsily along. A looby or fustilugs would go lumpering about.

LURCH

WILLIAM BLAKE sang of 'modest Dame Lurch who is always at Church', but lurch, on the whole, is not respectable. It has a great number of meanings, some of them discreditable. On the credit side, it is a game resembling back-gammon, or denotes a state of the score in which the winner is far ahead of the loser. Nothing amiss with that. But our ancestors were gamesmen as well as sportsmen and often played — yes, even cricket — to win because wagering had run high; they appeared to believe that you could not get a long lead fairly. For they gave lurch the meaning of swindle or cheat. It was also a trade-term of the Tudor 'spiv', since in 1568, it meant 'getting the start in obtaining food or profit'.

Lurch is also synonymous with lurk: honest loitering or lingering is distinct from lurching or lurking which nearly always implies mischievous purposes. 'I myself sometimes, leaving the fear of God on the left hand and hiding my honour in my necessity, am fain to shuffle, to hedge, and to lurch.' Thus Falstaff to Pistol who was standing on his honour with 'cat-a-mountain looks and red-lattice phrases'. A man who lurches in the familiar sense of staggering may well go 'stravaiging', as the Scots would say, on the windy side of the law. So Falstaff lurched.

Hedging, in this passage, means to go aside from the straight and narrow road of rectitude. A hedge-creeper was an old word for a rogue or lurcher. But hedge is also a blameless term for defend or protect; he who hedges a bet guards himself; he does not cheat the layer of the odds. Hedging, in the sense of refusing to make a decision or to commit oneself, presumably comes from the idea of taking cover. It is not evasion of the law, as Falstaff dodged and lurched; but it is evasion of responsibility, a deviation from the way of firmness and integrity. Hedging of this kind is the same as 'sitting on the fence', but I have heard no trimmer described as 'sitting on the hedge'. That practice would be too painful or at least too unrestful for the cautious and self-seeking man.

Use of the phrase, 'He had sat so long on the fence that the iron had entered into his soul' is now common. Naturally, for the thrust of its wit is powerful. But who invented it? The *Oxford Dictionary of Quotations* cannot help in tracing this masterly addition of the fence to the Psalmist's iron, which was originally linked with the misery of sitting in the stocks. I have been told that Lloyd George was the originator. If a trimmer is a stout and paunchy fellow, one might say of him that he has sat so long on the hedge that there is a crackling of thorns under the pot. Certainly it is true of certain politicians that they cannot see a fence without rushing to sit on it.

But we must return to lurching. The lurcher dog is not so called because he staggers — he is, as the Irishman said, very handy on his feet; he is a poacher's dog by definition, though he need not be so in fact. It is possible to be an honest mongrel and the lurcher was first a mongrel offspring of collie and greyhound. But he was used for the Falstaffian type of lurch and so got a bad name. This has taken us a long way from Blake's modest Dame, the regular church attender, good Mistress Lurch.

MACABRE

'Suffering is ugly', Norman Douglas has written. 'It was reserved for Christianity — Orientalism I should say — to discover its macabre fascination.' The history of that statement strikes me as dubious, but the use of macabre is pleasant. Macabre comes from the French, but, behind that, the ingenious lexicographers find a link with Maccabaeus. As a more imposing variant on gruesome it succeeds. The very sound of *danse macabre* hints at a shiver-some shuffle, an Apache's snatch-and-grab. Scottish history is such a gloomy medley of murder and theology, so fraught with ancient hate and future hell, that a Clan Macabre would seem symbolic of its fratricidal warfares and Calvinistic chronicles. One of the most macabre books in my experience is James Hogg's *Confessions of a Justified Sinner* which prophetically drives, by way of extreme Calvinism, into the very heart of modern Communism. The Lord's elect could do no wrong, since they were deemed to be inevitably heaven-bound. So can the chosen spirits of the Party justify any evil by the knowledge of their own dedication. Hogg, 'The Ettrick Shepherd', wrote a fair amount that was feeble and fey, but *The*

Confessions is a magnificent essay in the macabre and part of the required reading of our time.

MARASMUS

'EXCESS of application and some disgusts which are too often excited by envy of distinguished merit threw Mengs into a state of marasmus.' Marasmus is a decline due to wasting. The lean, jealous and over-worked Mengs was an eighteenth-century painter and draughtsman. The world of arts has always been full of marasmic types who, the more they dwindle in reputation, the more they grow in rancour. Young resentment of established and prosperous figures is a natural mood and those who girn at the success of others today will be the target of the same resentment tomorrow. It is the elderly marasmics, pining in disappointment, who achieve supremacy in the ranks of Club bores.

MAUFREY

A MAUFREY can drop its 'galli'. The following phrase (from a seventeenth-century expert in denunciation) 'to compolitize a multimonstrous maufrey of heteroclytes' is a rare piece of polysyllabic classicism. Multimonstrous is a useful adjective for a circus, menagerie, jungle, or for any raree-show in Nature or out of it. A heteroclyte, more commonly heteroclite, is an exceptional or anomalous person, a proper constituent of a multimonstrous maufrey. Gallimaufrey is attributed to the French galimafrée. The abbreviated maufrey seems to add to the note of contempt, suggesting the smallest fry of the least desirable kind. To compolitize is to bring into one society; our former League of Nations and present United Nations Organization have twice endeavoured to compolitize the peoples of the world. But unfortunately there is a maufrey of heteroclytes who have no desire to be assimilated or put under a reasonable discipline.

75

MELANGELL

THIS sounds half honey-sweet and half angelic. It is a saintly name and it is also used as a charm. I owe it to Eiluned Lewis's fresh, gay and informative rural diary called *Country Places*. Melangell was a princess who crossed from Ireland to Montgomery-shire and there established a sanctuary for wild life, probably the first of its kind.

> The land was granted her by a prince of Powis whose hounds had chased their quarry to the wooded valley where she was sheltering. So impressed was this prince by her power over all living animals, especially the little mountain hares, that he ordained that this particular valley should be kept as a perpetual sanctuary and no hare ever again be hunted there. In later, harsher times, Melangell would, doubtless, have been called a witch and either shunned or persecuted, but those were still the golden days of Christianity. She became a saint, pilgrims visited the valley where she died, and a church was built to her memory. It is still said that, if 'God and Melangell be with thee' is shouted after any hunted animal, it will escape.

I do not myself enjoy the pursuit of hares and my sympathies in the matter are Melangellite. It is hard to imagine a more beautiful message of clemency and good will than that beginning 'God and Melangell'.

METICULOSITY

'WITH the utmost meticulosity' is a recent pomposity for 'with the greatest care'. Meticulous is, I suppose, a word which has so completely changed its meaning that the proper one is almost wholly forgotten. Indeed, one of my dictionaries marks the definition 'timid' as 'obsolete'. Since a timid man may go warily, meticulous came to mean cautious, careful and then precise. So it has actually passed into the lingo of military communiqués. A meticulous commander is no longer a panicky one; he is a model of forethought.

As purveyors of turgid prose it would be hard to beat the generalissimo of today. Here is one example of what may be called MacArthurese. 'In defiance of all internationally recognized obligations of war declaration before initiating belligerency.'

So nobody starts a war now: they initiate belligerency. Further we read this justification from Tokio for 'the Command'. 'Both in the advance to the north and the subsequent withdrawals to the south its tactical deployments on the correctly assessed cold realities of the military situation as it actually developed have been meticulously according to the directive it was charged to implement.'

'Meticulously according to the directive it was charged to implement' is certainly an imposing variant on 'strictly according to orders'.

Exercise for students. Translate into War Office English (or American) the old brief phrase 'sealed orders'. The good examinee would, I suppose, introduce some polysyllabic Secret Directives demanding total meticulosity of implementation.

Since writing this I have noticed an American military order concerning fat men in the forces. They are termed 'obese personnel'. I shall remember that when next I see Falstaff on the stage.

MIFFY

In his admirable 'Marginal Comment' in *The Spectator* Harold Nicolson once wrote:

> I have been conscious on previous voyages to and from the United States that, whereas the approach to New York is unequalled in dramatic splendour, and whereas the Customs buildings on arrival were neat and well-arranged, our own front door was miffy and ill-kempt.

I had only vague ideas about the word miffy and so looked it up in *O.E.D.* A miff, I learned, is a 'fit of peevish ill-humour'. Arbuthnot wrote of Lady Harvey, 'She is in a little sort of a miff about a ballad that was wrote on her'. The verb miff has been used both transitively and intransitively for to give or take offence. ('To peeve' is perhaps our equivalent in modern slang.) Miffy, as an adjective, means touchy, easily offended. Mr. Nicolson employed it, apparently, to mean squalidly offensive: as such it seems to be his own invention — and a nice one. I do not feel miffy about his usage.

When I put this to Mr. Nicolson, he kindly allowed me to use his reply.

> I did not use the adjective 'miffy' to mean, as you suggest, 'squalidly offensive'. I used it merely to mean 'shabby'. No associations with the eighteenth-century meaning of the word were present in my mind. I have always heard the word used in horticultural parlance of plants which develop blackspot, or hang untidily and unproductively on their stalks. In this sense the word is used to mean something between 'sickly' or 'ragged'. I feel sure that horticulturalists would confirm this use of the word. But if I have invented this meaning I am not in the least repentant since the word conveys, in its tone of voice, exactly the impression which is needed. Of course it may be that the word is purely a family word which we have misused for years. We shall go on misusing it.

I like the Nicolsonian usage, agree that miffy sounds right for his meaning, and shall henceforth use miffy so.

MIZZLE

THIS word is so expressive that it has been used in many ways, of moist, drizzly rain, of slouching away or 'sloping off' and also, perhaps, as a verb meaning to confuse. 'Don't be mizzled by the next sign-post.' Was this utterance of an A.A. Motor Patrol a

corruption of misled or the past participle of a special verb to mizzle?
Certainly the latter seems to run naturally with rural English.
'He had me right mizzled with his mush of long words.' The
pompous prose of Criticese has often mizzled (and misled) a reader
struggling to discover what a Great Mind was endeavouring to
explain.

MUFFISHNESS

MRS. LYNN LYNTON, who wrote about the 'The Girl of
the Period' in *The Saturday Review* in the 1860s and is properly
quoted by Dr. Willett Cunnington in his anthology called *Women*,
observed of this creature — always behaving wrongly to the critics
of every age — that she painted her face and made unbounded
luxury her only aim.

> The Girl of the Period has done away with such moral muffish-
> ness as consideration for others, or regard for counsel and rebuke.
> It was all very well in old-fashioned times, when fathers and
> mothers had some authority and were treated with respect,
> to be tutored and made to obey, but she is far too fast and
> flourishing to be stopped in mid-career by these slow old
> morals; and as she lives to please herself, she does not care if
> she displeases every one else. . . .

Slow old morals presumably means decrepit moralists. Does the
word fast for raffish still survive? I never hear young men about
town called fast now, but I do hear financiers called swift.

Mrs. Lynton then added:

> If some fashionable *dévergondée en evidence* is reported to have
> come out with her dress below her shoulder blades, and a gold
> strap for all the sleeve thought necessary, the Girl of the Period
> follows suit next day; and then she wonders that men some-
> times mistake her for her prototype, or that mothers of girls
> not quite so far gone as herself refuse her as a companion for
> their daughters. . . .

Dévergondée en evidence is superb. Muffishness was a favourite Victorian term for softness and effeminacy. Since the muff at sports was one who caught a crab while rowing or missed 'a sitter' and got bowled for nothing at cricket, the muffish were 'softies'. Dean Farrar's schoolboys thought diligence at work a sign of this muffishness, just as Mrs. Lynton, a decade later in the same period, regarded muffishness as a favourite term of contempt among the brazen hussies whom she castigated for their mixture of paint and self-exposure.

A different kind of Muffishness or Muffism, as one authoress preferred to shorten it, was 'walking down St. James's Street on a gusty day in September, in a rough and somewhat shabby pilot coat'. That kind of muffishness became an honourable necessity in years of wars and poverty. To the peaceful, well-to-do Victorians this sartorial muffism was gaucherie comparable to failing at games or falling off a horse. It was scarcely the effeminacy which Dean Farrar and Mrs. Lynton associated with the word.

Muff, as a term of contempt, has a well-established place in English. I was puzzled by it while reading Marlowe's *Tamburlaine* which, though only recently restored to the stage, is an 'alms-basket of words'. Uribassa, who sounds like a bloated and choleric mixture of uric acid and bottled beer, exclaims:

> Besides, King Sigismund hath brought from Christendom
> More than his camp of stout Hungarians, —
> Sclavonians, Almains, Rutters, Muffs, and Danes,
> That with the halberd, lance, and murdering axe,
> Will hazard that we might with surety hold.

Marlowe was so pleased with the line beginning 'Sclavonians' that he repeated it, through the mouth of Orcanes, King of Natolia, shortly after, Muffs and all.

Muff was a term of contempt for Westphalians; then for Germans in general; then for all foreigners, including the Russians. Florio wrote of 'swaggering muffes or Dutchmen'. All nations have shown their racial contempts in monosyllabic dismissal of the supposedly minor breeds. The Americans, I fancy, invented 'Wop', the British 'Wog'. The Elizabethans took their pinch of snuff, shrugged their silken shoulders, and muttered 'Muff' as some alien boor trod on their toes or a curious fantastico went mincing on his way.

NAPPY

E V E R Y nursery knows what nappy means. So, at one time, did every beer-drinker. Nappy ale was strong and foaming. I notice in Sir Alfred Munning's vivid autobiography called *An Artist's Life* that he writes of nappy horses. This might mean that they are unclipped and carried a thick 'nap', but from the context it is plain that he means heady, frisky, restive. As such it is a good, liquorish term. Is it carried to the card-room and the game of Nap, in which a bold declarer would naturally be nappy?

NAUGHTY-PACK

I T is a curious habit to disparage one's fellow-humans in terms of parcels and luggage. Restoration comedy is full of young women dismissed as baggages; pack or naughty-pack was similarly employed. Perhaps it is natural for men with a load of feminine mischief to think in terms of a burdensome portmanteau or valise. Of these porterage terms of playful abuse I think pack is even better than baggage. 'Hence, pack' is a brief and effective dismissal. A correspondent reminds me of hearing the word 'bluggage' used by a distraught young woman who wished to discover her 'grips' among a vast pile of trunks and bags on a railway platform. 'Where's my bluggage?' certainly indicates an urge for the expletive among the major pains of travel. Bluggage, too, might be picturesquely and feelingly applied to the feminine baggage or naughty-pack.

NIGROGLOBULATE

T H E English gentleman's sport of throwing black-balls at potential members of his club evoked this delightful word. One who had proposed a candidate over whose social merits there was some dispute heard by wire that all was well. The dark missiles had not been hurled. He replied

> Across the wires the electric message ran
> They did not nigroglobulate my man.

Personally I regard this business of nigroglobulation childish and silly. But the invented word is a sweet monster.

NOCTURNE

N E W S has been sent to me by the far-travelled, word-relishing, and phrase-vigilant Stewart Perowne that an electric sign in a dingy part of Treviso announces 'Hot Club Notturno'. This started reflection on the horrid usages of the word hot, which is ugly enough in any case, and on the beauty of the word nocturne. 'An instrumental composition of a dreamy character, expressive of sentiment appropriate to evening or night.' A serenade, then, is for voices, a nocturne for the wood-wind and the strings. But to me the word nocturne rises above the gentle dismissal of the dictionary. It is as great as Whistler, who gave thanks for the term. It has the immensity as well as the dreaminess of night. The adjective nocturnal is a good Thomas Hardy word,

> In nocturnal blackness, mothy and warm,
> When the hedgehog travels furtively over the lawn,

No doubt the Hot Club Notturno is mothy and warm too. One can visualize the flutterings round its pink lampshades.

The syllable 'noct' is ugly, but the roll of the 'ur' brings, as usual, a rich dignity. I cannot think of a nocturne as being trivial. It is large enough for Chopin and Whistler and Keats and is not 'just a song at twilight'. Serenade flatters this last. Nocturnity (if the word did not exist, I insist that it does now) is full of the 'verdurous glooms' and 'embalmed darkness' into which Keats peered in rapture while he listened beside his mulberry tree. I will not have nocturne relegated to musical-comedy tenors and sea-front pierrots fluting of Thora and similar evasive fair ones with eyes of blue and hands as pale as daisies.

In the days when it was fashionable to give novels one word names, e.g., Compton Mackenzie's *Carnival*, Frank Swinnerton wrote a fine one called *Nocturne* which, like *She Stoops to Conquer*, dealt with 'The Accidents of a Night'. It makes an excellent, nerve-tingling title, whether for painting, writing, or music. Or even for a hat. 'Max', on Dandies, observed that, while Jerome K. Jerome's bowler was a perfect preface to all his works, 'the silk hat of Mr. Whistler is a real nocturne and his linen a symphony *en blanc majeur*'.

The Latin *nox* and *lux* are not attractive nouns: we certainly improve on them with night and light. Why does one shudder at the spelling nite? I am sure the Hot Club Notturno is also a Nitery. I see the word Nite now written up in the environs of Leicester Square: like the announcement of Sox and Snax it always infuriates me, but really without logic. Our ght's are justified only by association and tradition. But to many people these are much more than logic. The adjectives coming from *nox* and *lux*, nocturnal and lucid, are worthy of the elemental beauties. What of tenebrous for nocturnal? Or of tenebrious or tenebrific since both exist? A trifle pedantic? Scarcely, since Carlyle actually wrote of 'books done by pedants and tenebrific persons under the name of men'. That dismissal is as much to my liking as the authors, mistily superior amid their word-tangles, are not. Nocturnal is too kind a term for the darkness of some contemporary writing in prose and verse: the stuff is tenebrific.

NUTS

'In the course of the discussion at the Royal Institution of Chartered Surveyors on Mr. W. R. Brackett's Paper on development charges, Mr. W. E. A. Bull (Member of Council) said he found the greatest difficulty in understanding the development charge regulations; they were as difficult to understand as that other regulation which had received some publicity recently, which read: 'In the Nuts (Unground) other than Groundnuts Order, the expression "nuts" shall have reference to such nuts other than groundnuts as would, apart from this Amending Order, fail to qualify as nuts (unground)' (*The Estates Gazette*, February 3rd, 1951).

Crack that one.

OPOPANAX

'Patchouli and opopanax — what are they anyway? Does anyone know?' How charming to find a journalist beginning with a confession of complete ignorance: also of under-equipment. Has he no dictionary? (I shall not therefore name him.) Did the inquirer possess some lexicon he would realize that the two last syllables of opopanax are the same as the word panacea, cure-all. Opos is juice and the whole a potent, juicy salve. Yet the lexicographer, having offered so beneficent an article, then adds gloomily 'A fetid gum-resin'. Then he cheers up a little and adds that it is a resin from Balsamodendron useful in perfumery. (What a noble end to an hexameter could Balsomodendron be!) After that he descends to the material consideration of opopanactic soap.

Patchouli is 'an odoriferous plant native to the Malay Peninsula, yielding an essential oil from which scent is made'. So now we know and can give precise answers when we run into the various elements of a fop's pomatum-cupboard in, perhaps, one of Sir Max

Beerbohm's deliciously dandiacal essays on dandies and dandyism.

Since Poetry, at least in the person of Christopher Fry, has returned to the enjoyment and employment of flowery and aromatic words I think we may still meet a new Orsino in one of his plays, an exquisite baronial figure, patchouli'd and opopanactic. And should any of our bards ever resort to the pastime of Clough and Tennyson and compose English hexameters then surely

Essences suave he drew from his boskage of Balsamodendron

would suit the occasion.

OSTRICH

THIS word, I gather, is a popular corruption of avis-struthio, reaching us through the French autruche. (How, by the way, do the Scottish Highlands produce a clan of McOstrich; of what is that a derivative?) I was reminded of the ostrich by finding, amid the awe-inspiring terminology of the British Medical Journal, a simple headline, 'Human Ostrich'. A sufferer from extreme stomach trouble was found to have swallowed a bicycle spanner, a steel twist-drill and part of a hack-saw. He seems to have worked hard to obtain his affliction.

> Was it for honour he did it
> Or rather for reasons of pelf?
> Or simply because an acquaintance
> Had said 'Go and murder yourself!'

Human ostrich, as I said, struck my eye by its quiet use of English in a publication written mainly in the classic jargon so assiduously cultivated by doctors. Why is a swelling always an oedema? Why are patients able to walk always described as ambulants? Why is feeling the sore spot called 'bimanual palpation'? All professions like to pretend that they are masters of a mystery and the lawyers rival the doctors in spreading the veil of obscurity over all their processes.

I can hardly recommend the *B.M.J.* for general reading, however great its value to the masters of medical craft, since the laity, as it calls us, will immediately be driven into intense panic and imagine that they are suffering from every physical horror under the sun — or the X-Ray. What a contents bill is this which leads off with Somatrophic Hormone in Production of Malignant Nephrosclerosis, Periarteritis Nodose, and Hypertensive Disease and passes on to Torsion of the Great Omentum and Haemolytic Transfusion Reaction due to an Anti-Lewis Agglutinin. (What had Lewis done to be thus agglutinized? Seemingly he was in the right.) I cannot help wondering, as I thumb my way nervously through terms like 'electrophoretically', whether the average G.P. — the kind of genial man you meet in the golf-club having a whisky after his rounds — really understands much of what the sages of research are telling him in their portentous dog-Greek and high-piled Latinity. I once had a fairly rigorous dosage of Latin and Greek literature, and so I do start a point or two up on most doctors, who were not as a rule intensively trained in the classics. But many of the polysyllables defeat me, despite that schooling. Has Doctor Pat O'Golly, that amiable clubman who is so popular everywhere, more than an inkling as to what all this means? Could he translate 'Propylene glycol alone does not affect the eosinophil level'? Perhaps not. And he, as well as I, may be relieved to come across, amid all this, a plain Human Ostrich.

OVERBURDEN

EVEN such a spoliation of land as open-cast mining can produce a touch of poetry. I learn that the crust of a mine cut out and folded over the surface of adjacent soil is called an overburden. I do not know how far the poets have profited by the sonorous appeal of spirits overburdened.

> Hush, if you saw some western cloud
> All billowy-bosomed, over-bowed
> By many benedictions — sun's
> And moon's and evening star's at once —

Perhaps Browning made use of overburden too. It is both a lyrical and a sonnet-worthy adjective.

Burden, a thing borne, itself possesses a fine roll of endurance in its first syllable. 'The burden and heat of the day' (usually misquoted as 'heat and burden of the day') are heavy, sweltering words, with torpor hinted. Put over before burden and the gravity of toil acquires beauty of sound as well.

PALSY

THE aged Duke of York in *Richard II* calls his right arm 'now prisoner to a palsy'. Palsy is an inspired abbreviation; it is really paralysis. 'Sick of a palsy' strikes at compassion in a way that paralysis does not and palsied age is far more moving than paralytic decrepitude. Sir John Squire amusingly exemplified, in his book *Flowers of Speech*, the potential beauty of the doctor's lingo. In a brilliant Tennysonian and Shakespearean pastiche he wrote,

> How long ago upon the fabulous shores
> Of far Lumbago, all a summer's day,
> He and the maid Neuralgia, they twain,
> Lay in a flower-crowned mead, and garlands wove,
> Of gout and yellow hydrocephaly,
> Dim palsies, pyorrhoea and the sweet
> Myopia, bluer than the summer sky,
> Agues both white and red, pied common cold,
> Cirrhosis, and that wan, faint flower of love
> The shepherds call dyspepsia.

It is worth noting, that unlike the modern reporter, he uses fabulous correctly. But the game can be played both ways. Why not a witches' coven of infirmities and blains? Might it not too be versified?

> What time the hag Psoriasis uprose,
> Beckoned her pocky train and called the roll,
> Mumpish Oedema, Tetter, Shingles, Scab,
> Old Beldam Rheum and slavering Catarrh,
> With necklet of carbuncles, warts, and scabs,
> Most loathsome of all Lucifer's regalia,
> Itch, Abscess, Flux and bloated Imposthume.

No, we cannot let Sir John have it all his own way, though he does well to enlist on beauty's side, Impetigo, Scrofula and Eczema, in earlier lines not quoted. I was gratified by his use of Palsy, which is far too good a word for my atrocious assembly and quivered tenderly in his catalogue of charming maladies, his dream of fair plagues.

PARK

THE Greek Paradise meant a park. The word was promoted by Christianity to the loftiest of meanings. Paradise soared upwards, park sank down. It has dwindled from being an enclosed forest or chase to serving as a legal receptacle for motor-cars. This usage came from the military parks where stores, waggons and munitions were enclosed. The Scots have retained park to signify a fenced field.

> Binder and reaper clattered and wheeped through the brittle weather that held the Howe, soon the weather would break and the stooking was far behind in Blawearie. Father would wander out by the biggins and stare at the parks . . . Kinraddie slept like a place in a picture-book, drifting long shadows that danced a petronella across the night-stilled parks. (From *Sunset Song* by Lewis Grassic Gibbon.)

That author's lyrical prose-pictures of Angus and the Mearns and his salty realism of that crofter-folk is rich in parks where poor men chaved (toiled) amid beauty that gave them little except the chaving.

Parks remained, in richer England, private demesnes and ornamental lands; then they dismally became, under urban necessity, little used squares and streets or dusty bomb-sites turned over to stationary traffic. Park has touched the heights of rural amenity and plumbed the lower depths of urban utility. It has been sweetly scented with flowers ungathered or with new-mown hay. It has become odious with fumes and the din of 'revving-up'. 'In a park where the peach-blossoms blew', sang Andrew Lang of the reign of the Emperor Hwang. 'Over pale, over park' flew Puck, among the enchanted airs of the Athenian forest. 'Can I park here?' we inquire, having found an urban void or a machine-packed yard beside the litter-bins of a 'beauty-spot'.

PATTERAN

KIPLING knew the argot for a gipsy trail.

> Follow the Romany patteran
> North where the blue bergs sail,

Patteran, or more commonly patrin, is a line of journey, marked by signs; in the case of the gypsies it is usually signified by tufts of grass. The three-syllabled patteran suits the poet's rhythm better than patrin when he wishes to describe places where the caravan has rested or passed on. Do young runners still play 'Hare and Hounds' with a patteran of torn paper? Perhaps conscience about the messing-up of the countryside has diminished this sport. Good school-boys do not wish to be litterers, for whom by the way, litter-bugs would surely be a good term and in the manner of our time. It would flatter the 'mucky pups' of the picnic debris to call them patteraners.

PICAYUNE

THE American influence on our high-brow writers may work
well enough sometimes, since America has kept so many old and
excellent words which we have lost. But I see no point in the
usage of a lofty left-wing English critic who dismisses a London
play as picayune. How many of his readers, if he has any, know
that a picayune is an old American name for a five-cent piece?
It therefore signifies trifling or next to worthless. It is a legitimate,
as well as a picturesque word, when offered to a public which knows
what it means. But to use it in London is a tiresome form of verbal
foppery. The same writer, I see, used aficionado when he means
admirer. This type of affectation has been properly ridiculed by
Ogden Nash in one of his *New Yorker* rhymes. My lofty friend
should become an aficionado of the *New Yorker*. It contains far
better English than he manages to write.

PLATYPOD

THOSE afflicted with fallen arches may, if it relieves them, call
themselves platypods. But I cannot think that to put a classical name
on a distress is really to provide a salve. The song about Aberdeen's
Jean ('Though we know your feet are flat, you are none the worse
for that') would not be more complimentary if it concerned a
reference to a Deeside platypod. I have been reading a book on
Golf advocating 'The Flat Foot Method', especially for the seniors
and the stout. They are to be platypods when addressing the ball
and abjure all tip-toe graces and all attempts at an elongated swing.
Let them get right down to it, eyes on the ball and toes well dug in.
I suggest platypodgily as the cautionary word for golfers with a
middle-aged spread.

The great J. H. Taylor has told me that he preferred playing the
game in 'boots of an agricultural character'. They assisted the

downward pressure, the platypodosity which guarantees balance
in the stance and accuracy in the stroke. No ballet-dancing on the
tee for him. And none, either, for the propounder of the Flatfoot
way. Although an American and a theorist, he surprised me by
avoiding Grecian polysyllables. He is no platypod in self-description
but whacks his way to victory as a Flattie, to use the term rudely
applied to the Police; unjustly too, for some of our younger con-
stables look so lithe and agile that you would think they were
trained at Sadler's Wells.

POMMLE

P O M M E L is a round knob as well as the projecting front part of
a saddle; so it may be anything circular, like a ball. John Masefield
has used it as an adjective for corpulent (with a slightly altered
spelling). To the meet of hounds, in *Reynard the Fox*

> A pommle cob came trotting up,
> Round-bellied like a drinking-cup,
> Bearing on back a pommle man,
> Round-bellied like a drinking can,
> The clergyman from Condicote. . . .

A similar word of knob-like significance is Cascabel. This too
would make an adjective and one of some charm, worthy at any
rate of a robust Rubens goddess. Or might the adjective be Casca-
belline? No, that is a trifle too handsome for the plump. One can
imagine both words in a poem of the Stephen Phillips school.

> Then came the pommle burghers to the feast
> With consorts cascabel.

The latter word adds dignity to adiposity and there is a nice air
of rubious health about pommle, with no suggestion of a sallow
and a morbid fat.

PROCESS

O N C E a word becomes fashionable there is no limit to the eagerness to use it. Take, for example, the verb 'to process', now commonly applied to foods which have been moulded, messed about and comprehensively robbed of their true flavour and character. (I have no interest in 'processed cheese'.) A fresh and somewhat startling use of this verb occurred recently in the American magazine *Life*, International Edition, January 1st, 1951. 'The harem where Abdul (Hamid II) processed an estimated 30,000 women during his lifetime'. And who, by the way, was the estimator?

PROMULGATE

N E W S of a court-martial is always followed by the statement that 'Sentence will be promulgated in due course'. Laws are occasionally promulgated, sentences always. Why cannot they be announced? Presumably there is thought to be more dignity and authority about promulgation. If Judges do not vulgarly agree but more formally concur, then the grim result of the concurrence must be suitably phrased. So promulgation continues. These heavy Latinities continue to give satisfaction. Story-tellers obviously gather self-confidence if they say 'At that juncture' instead of 'Then'. But could anything be more absurdly pompous than their juncture? Cannot we promulgate a sentence of banishment upon it?

At this juncture, by the way, I have just noticed that some committee of mandarins in our economic world is going to promulgate a new wages structure for an industry. No well-conducted citizen of today asks simply for more money. He demands a revision of the wages structure in his field of labour and is told that the said wages structure is 'constantly under review'.

PROPAGATE

SAID Romeo

> Griefs of my own lie heavy in my breast
> Which thou wilt propagate.

He is close here to the original meaning of propagate, 'to fasten or peg down slips of plants for growth, to multiply plants by layering'. Hence it later meant to breed one's kind and later still to diffuse one's news. And so to the ever-present propaganda. I hate using the word propaganda, but it is now very difficult to avoid.

Propaganda in our time suggests dishonest persuasion, yet it had a most august and holy start in life, when Pope Gregory XV founded his Commission of Cardinals as a *Congregatio De Propaganda Fide*. For the word was first applied to persons or systems rather than to doctrinal instruction. 'Any association, systematic scheme, or concerted movement for the propagation of a particular doctrine or practice' is one of the definitions. In our time propaganda has become impersonal and signifies chiefly the ideas propagated and the process of propagation. Hence, by back-formation, the verb to propagand, which is a sorry use of the original Latin, if you wish to be strict in these matters. It should, of course, be propagate; but that has become chiefly physical in meaning.

Propaganda is now mainly a political word and it is a calamitous tribute to the high art and craft of statesmanship that political propaganda has acquired a bad smell. We began with the innocence of plants, we moved to the sacred missionary purposes of the Vatican, and we end with the shifty cozenage of politicians' manœuvres. I admit that propaganda can still be used of honourable persuasion, but as a rule it suggests a certain measure of deceit, if not downright dishonesty (e.g. 'That's just propaganda', which is scarcely a compliment).

There are plenty of slang terms for propaganda now. I note that an outburst of propagandist statements by Stalin was dismissed by an American Senator as 'The old malarkey'. I have no idea what malarkey actually signifies. Damon Runyon's Broadway argot included 'the old phedinkus', which has a Grecian savour. Malarkey, in the same way, has a Latin-sounding first syllable. When the narrator of one of Runyon's admirable tales observed in Mindy's restaurant that he was afflicted with the tender passion, the 'I' of the story confessed that 'For me love is just the old phedinkus'. The same voice often spoke of 'the phonus bolonus' and I surmise that phedinkus meant much the same to him and that malarkey is cousin to boloney and phedinkus too.

Boloney comes from the famous Bologna sausage and was Polony in Cockney usage: then it still meant a reputable sausage, but the American boloney refers to malarkey and phedinkus, not to honest pork. Just as propaganda has fallen from the affairs of faith to the less desirable works of the politician, so has tasty sausage-meat descended to the status of a fraud. Phonus Bolonus is the ultimate fate of the gardener's honourable propagation.

PURPUREAL

H O R A C E permitted the 'purple patch' to colour writing of grave purpose and great profession. That was the *purpureus pannus* and the English adjective purpureal sometimes supplants the shorter purple — and to advantage.

> Of all that it is most beauteous — imaged there
> In happier beauty, more pellucid streams,
> An ampler ether, a diviner air,
> And fields invested with purpureal gleams.

Those are not the best lines in Wordsworth's *Laodamia* which contains

> The gods approve
> The depth, and not the tumult, of the soul.

But purpureal gleams are better to the ear than purple ones. There is something wrong with the word purple: surely it is inadequate to symbolize majesty and triumph. It is all very well for blood-pressure folk.

> Art thou a Man of purple cheer,
> A rosy Man, right plump to see?

Purple is satisfactory in that verse of Wordsworth's epitaph for a Poet, with its contempt both for the sensual world, the moralist, and the 'intellectual All-in-All'. Cheer of this facial kind could hardly be purpureal. But gleams in an ampler ether and diviner air may well be rewarded with the two extra syllables. The Byronic cohorts of the Assyrian might have been purpureal too. Purple patches will do for prose; purpureal will assist the poet who does not care for a loquitive style.

REGALE

W H Y have we dropped the use of regale as a noun? At Inverary, where it rained so hard — as usual — that Dr. Johnson drank a gill of whisky, all but a drop, though he had previously taken no alcohol all through his arduous and often rain-swept tour, Boswell found 'a letter from Mr. Garrick which was a regale as agreeable as a pine-apple would be in a desert'. Horace Walpole wrote of being 'threatened with a regale of hams', which seems no appalling menace nowadays. The verb regale has became associated with the more pretentious kind of children's story book. No doubt the Marquess of Carabbas regaled himself with a cold collation. But a regale makes an appetizing noun. It is a cooler form of the refocillants — warmers of the internal hearth — mentioned by John Aubrey. Let us once more have a regale of pine-apple for a sultry fatigue and a refocillating glass against a shivering depression.

ROUT

T H E R E are caterers of such decent antiquity that they still claim in their literature of advertisement to supply the viands and cordials proper to a rout. Nobody, of course, throws a rout nowadays, but why, I have wondered, do people throw parties, as if they were English cricket-balls or Scottish cabers. The latter, I know, are tossed; parties, too, might be tossed, possibly a better word for the hilarious occasion than the more sober thrown.

The modern rout (or party) was originally 'thrown' by Americans. The American Thesaurus of Slang suggests that thrown parties 'are associations of the sexes where the exchange of caresses is the chief amusement'. But in England we are more austere; you can still throw a party with no expectation of a 'necking' or 'petting' orgy. Conversation, eased by alcohol, generally suffices.

The vocabulary of catering and hospitality has, even now, its pleasant features. Cafeteria, for example, with which the high cost of service has made the British more familiar, is quite a beautiful word. One can imagine it in the statelier blank verse.

> Rich and abundant cates
> The cosmic cafeteria displays
> For those who pick, with shrewd, selective eye,
> Life's delicate provision.

It is always nice, in the leanest times, to hear of a firm's Banqueting Department. Banquet sounds so bountiful, even when the reality is but a meagre meal with a deluge of bad speeches to follow. Waiters who spend their summers at holiday hotels may return from the seaside to the city to hibernate on their savings, helped out with the rewards of 'Banqueting work', an august title for casual service of the Masons and other dining fraternities on one or two evenings a week.

The antique rout had its own terminology; rout-seats were the folding chairs hired out for the big assemblies or 'do's. And there were pastries and cakes called rout-cakes; these Joseph Sedley could consume in bulk. After the curry to which the Sedleys entertained Becky Sharp, there was more to come. 'Being an invalid Joseph Sedley contented himself at dinner with a bottle of claret besides his Madeira and he managed a couple of platefuls of strawberries and cream and twenty-four rout-cakes that were lying neglected', after which considerable feat he still had energy to go and see the Forty Thieves and Miss Decamps's dance.

There is something to be said for the simple, vernacular 'do' as a description of the modern rout. I have not forgotten a revue sketch of many years ago in which Gracie Fields played a raw north-country girl brought into help at a suburban dinner. While the table was being laid the hostess told her to lay wine-glasses. 'Ee, wine!' said Gracie with a glint in her eye, 'Wine! Going to be a droonken do!'

SALARIAT

I was asked 'What is the use of talking about the Middle Class, when there has ceased to be an Upper Class?' I suppose the term is moribund, or even dead. If the Upper Class has departed, and if there is no reality in talking about a Lower Class, then there is no sense in trying to retain a Middle Class. The sectionalized Victorian society could make further distinctions. 'Bow, bow, ye Lower Middle Classes.' At what point did Lower Middle become Upper Middle — or Middle Middle? But there is some place for the word salariat, which arrived in 1918, according to the dictionary, as a contrast to proletariat. The salaried man, who draws his rewards at longer intervals than the wage-earner or piece-worker, has rather more security and a slightly different status. But salariat is not much used, whereas the undefinable and now disappearing Middle Class still are spoken of as such. The old words were clerisy for educated folk and menalty for those of middle social rank. I think salariat best replaces them, if replaced they must be.

Both proletariat and salariat have queer Roman origins. The proletarians were the lowest class in the Roman state, sardonically supposed to contribute nothing but their 'proles' or offspring to the common weal; the salary was the salt-money paid to a Roman soldier, a fixed and regular payment.

SCARLET

'Y E daughters of Israel, weep over Saul, who clothed you in scarlet, with other delights.' The translators of the Bible took a considerable relish in scarlet, an Oriental word which we owe to Persia, a word, also, which has a richness proper to its meaning. To the translators it was often emblematic of that luxury which, for austere prophets, was the road to ruin. To wear scarlet was to be a candidate for downfall. 'They that feed delicately are desolate in the streets; they that were brought up in scarlet embrace dung-hills.' (Surely 'feed' should be 'fed'.) Thus the author of 'Lamentations', who, in translation, was given a curious knack of pouring his woe into a resemblance of Latin hexameters.

> Our skin was black like an oven because of the terrible famine.
> They ravished the women in Zion and the maids in the cities
> of Judah.

In 'Revelations' the 'great whore', with whom the kings of the earth had committed fornication, sat upon a seven-headed, ten-horned scarlet beast and was arrayed in purple and scarlet. To be clad merely in red would have been inadequate for 'the Mother of Harlots and Abominations of the Earth'. The 'Song of Solomon' attributed to the black but comely charmer teeth like sheep shorn and newly washed, hair like the goats on Gilead, and lips like a thread of scarlet. The first two compliments suggest a shepherd's delight, the third a courtier's beauty. Scarlet goes with the high places, not of the mountains, but of state and pomp. Romeo's first love Rosaline resembled Solomon's ideal not least in what Scots call 'the mou'. At least Mercutio saw her so,

> I conjure thee by Rosaline's bright eyes,
> By her high forehead and her scarlet lip,
> By her fine foot, straight leg, and quivering thigh —

Crimson, also an Oriental, is a beautiful word but it has less suggestion of a baleful blaze. Rosaline in life had scarlet lips; of Juliet in death Romeo cried

> Beauty's ensign yet
> Is crimson in thy lips and in thy cheeks.

It is true that in 'Isaiah' sins are described as crimson, but surely scarlet suits them better. The Great Whore could never have ridden crimson-robed upon a crimson Beast.

SCURREYER

A SCURREYER is old English for a member of a quick-moving patrol, sent out on a scouting expedition. Presumably the term telescoped scurry and survey, that is if the accent was put on the second syllable, as it well might be in heroic verse.

> Send forth scurreyers who, with falcon's eye,
> And speed no less, descending from our heights. . . .

Descending from this poetic eminence I come to snootle, which has been recommended to me as a happy marriage of tootle and snoop. It was applied by an Admiral to a Press Photographer who was doing a bit of private scurreying by rushing round the docks on a motor-bicycle. His attempt to penetrate some naval mysteries was met with a peremptory roar of 'You can't go snootling here'.

The Press Photographer probably thought the Admiral 'snooty', a nicely expressive piece of slang which has no dictionary status.

SCURRYFUNGE

B U T we are not finished with scurry-work yet.

Here is an extract from a letter of William Cowper to Lady Hesketh.

> I know not my dearest Coz that I have anything to trouble thee about save half a dozen tooth-brushes; Mrs. Unwin will be much obliged to thee also for a black Summer cloak *untrimm'd*, because Hannah is making a trimming for it. Two of the brushes abovesaid must be for inside scurryfunging, viz — they must be *hook'd*. These wants satisfied, we have no other commissions with which to charge thee. The stiffer the brushes the better.

I know no history of the tooth-brush: if it does not exist, it should be written. I expected a chronicle of tooth-scrubbing in the *History of Everyday Things in England* by Marjorie and C. H. B. Quennell, but could not find one.

Scurryfunging, with its suggestion of scraping away fungus, is a fine, grim term for dental scouring and suits the stiff, hooked article for which Cowper asked. It is interesting to note that there were then different species of brush available: he wanted two of the potent scurryfungers and four other, presumably gentler, weapons.

SHADES AND SHADOW

T H E S E symbols of dark, sad and transient things naturally crowd our poetry and the latter word especially adorns it. It is strange that the extra syllable should add so much poignancy, but certainly it does so. The meaning of the two is sometimes, but not essentially, the same. Shadows are what the shade creates, but, in fancy, much more. A shade can be a ghost.

And oft between the boughs is seen
The sly shade of a Rural Dean.

A Dean's shadow would be that of a living man. So from this
spectral suggestion 'the shades' became a synonym for the lower
world or Hades. And for that reason, I suppose, the word lingers
above the cellars of elderly taverns, which still occasionally invite
your descent to their Avernus, The Shades. These, I think, always
signify an underground 'snug'.

'Man walketh in a vain shadow.' 'What shadows we are and
what shadows we pursue.' Substitute shade for shadow and the
feeling is lost. The final -ow contributes powerfully to the idea
of futility and evanescence. 'He has outsoared the shadow of our
night', sang Shelley over Adonais, secure, so soon, from the con-
tagion of the world's slow stain. The second syllable of shadow not
only helps the scansion. It tolls the bell.

Shadow was a particular favourite with Shakespeare. It was not
only a technical name for the covered part of his stage: it declared
his notion of his own profession's unreality, but not, for that
reason, of its inutility. Art, especially theatrical art, is a shadowing
of life and the shadow is perhaps more beautiful and moving than
life itself, as the shadows of evening are often more beautiful than
the bright radiance of the day. When the Athenian rustics are acting
their rough comedy at the end of *A Midsummer Night's Dream*
Duke Theseus rebukes some boorish mockery of the mummers by
saying, 'The best in this kind are but shadows — and the worst are
no worse if imagination amend them'. There is a whole philosophy
in that astonishing sentence, 'The best in this kind are but shadows!'
Remember that, Master Kemp. Take heed of your ephemeral
calling, Master Burbage. And again, in the epilogue, when Puck
begins the actor's apology with

If we shadows have offended

the word, with its picturing of dim, thin creatures flitting in their
insubstantial pageant, tears at the heart. Macbeth, too, mingled it
with the player's impermanent craft,

> Life's but a walking shadow, a poor player,
> That struts and frets his hour upon the stage,
> And then is heard no more.

Then there is the haunting beauty of Sonnet 53.

> What is your substance, whereof you are made,
> That millions of strange shadows on you tend?
> Since every one hath, every one, one shade,
> And you, but one, can every shadow lend.
> Describe Adonis and the counterfeit
> Is poorly imitated after you;
> On Helen's cheek all art of beauty set,
> And you in Grecian tires are painted new.
> Speak of the spring, and foison of the year;
> The one doth shadow of your beauty show,
> The other as your bounty doth appear;
> And you in every blessed shape we know,
> In all external grace you have some part,
> But you like none, none you, for constant heart.

Oscar Wilde cited these lines in support of his view that the recipient was an actor. But no actor plays millions of parts and that first couplet remains as baffling as it is beautiful. Yet the general intention of flattery without loss of dignity is plain.

Shakespeare was constantly playing with the word shadow,

> For since the substance of your perfect self
> Is else devoted, I am but a shadow
> And to your shadow will I make true love.

That is spoken by Proteus in *The Two Gentlemen of Verona*, but its sentiment might occur in the Sonnets. Shadow for him was an attractive because an elastic word; it has itself so many shadows as well as shades of meaning.

Cleopatra, when becoming philosophical in the praise of her dead lord, cried out

> Nature wants stuff
> To vie strange forms with fancy: yet t'imagine
> An Antony, were nature's piece 'gainst fancy,
> Condemning shadows quite.

Shadows here are the creations of the artist, which natural man, in miraculously begetting an Antony, has far outranged. But they were also shades or ghosts;

> then came wandering by
> A shadow, like an angel, with bright hair.

Shadows are actors and spectres, creations of the mind and even, in the person of Simon Shadow and his fellow-conscripts, faint copies of the martial man. Sir Thomas Browne summed up the inclusiveness of shadows.

> Life itself is but a shadow of death and souls departed but the shadows of the living. All things fall under this name. The sun itself is but the dark *simulacrum* and light but the shadow of God.

The word shadow has thrown infinite magic upon our literature.

SICCITY

DR. JOHNSON admitted this Latin term for dryness: we now retain desiccated, but have abandoned the noun, which seems to me very apt in sound and in look. (Mr. Churchill might revive it. 'The deplorable siccity of taste and thought displayed by the Honourable Member'.) The siccity of a preacher's sermon is the right word for aridity of discourse. Johnson also used the adjective desiccative. Reviewing Mr. Hanway's peevish tirade on the miseries and mischiefs of tea-drinking, Johnson disputed the view that 'tea is a desiccative and ought not to be used after the fortieth year'. He explains that he, without desiccation, has 'long exceeded those limits of permission' and adds 'If tea be desiccative it cannot weaken the fibres, as our author imagines; if it be emetic, it must constringe the stomach, rather than relax it'. Mr. Hanway's siccity of mind in analysing the vices of tea-drinking was exposed in that review, but the Doctor, though an addict, dismissed tea with less courtesy than it merits. 'As it neither exhilarates the mind nor stimulates the palate, it is commonly an entertainment merely nominal, a pretext for assembling to parties, for interrupting business or diversifying idleness.' This is surely a very desiccated description of the cup and its power to cheer. What is business for except to be agreeably interrupted and, if idleness there be, is it not better diversified by the old Bohea, or the new Assam and Ceylon than left in dry monotony, a siccity of mind as of throat?

SIMPLY

WHAT a queer fate has overtaken simply! Put in front of a verb or participle it now means merely or solely. 'He simply said' is something quite different from 'he said simply'. I was reminded of this by Milton's description of the Shepherds in his 'Hymn on the Morning of Christ's Nativity'.

> The Shepherds on the Lawn
> Or ere the point of dawn
> Sate simply chatting in a rustick row.

In our modern idiom that implies that they should have been doing something more than sit and gossip. But there was no censure in Milton for their blameless conversation.

Great variety of meaning has overtaken simple, which has meant both honest and half-witted, unaffected and uncomplicated, sincere and easy. The word seems to speak innocence by its very sound. 'The short and simple annals of the poor.' You can hardly believe, after reading such a line, that any poor man ever got his affairs in a tangle, loved more often than lawfully, or deviated from the truth: which simply is not true.

SLAISTER

T H E word is not much used in England, but it may have a hold in the North as well as in Scotland. A slaistery thing is unctuous and defiling. To slaister is to paint or colour ill. Vulgar little vamps slaister their faces. It gives a rich and odious suggestion of bad, greasy make-up and of lips crudely incarnadined; also of vulgar decoration of a room or person. To call wet, mud-making weather slaistery seems almost flattering to the adjective. A slaister-kyte is a foul feeder. I thank 'Ximenes' of the *Observer* for bringing slaistered into one of his puzzles; it deserves to be more widely known and used.

What is the Southern English equivalent? Bedaubed is not nearly so effective, since slaistered suggests the slap-dash use of paint in a showy or sluttish way. I made previous mention of the adjective bejezebelled; that is a more portentous form of slaistered. A person of some quality who has overdone her preparation for conquest could be accused of bejezebellery; but no person of any quality could be slaistered. It is a word for wantons of the meaner sort.

SLAP-BANG

A S H O P where you have to put your cash on the counter. 'Please do not ask for credit as a refusal often annoys'; thus the printed notice sometimes politely announces policy, a most courteous deterrent to the hunter of 'tick' in a slap-bang shop or tavern. Tick, presumed to be short for ticket, is a reputable, dictionary word and not merely slang. Tally, I think, is little used now. I remember attending a music-hall in my youth, where Little Tich, as he skipped and pranced on his elongated boots, sang a song about a Tallyman. I did not know what a tallyman was, but it soon became obvious that a tallyman went round dealing on credit and strenuously endeavoured to collect later on the amount due on the tallies or marks. He was the direct opposite of a slap-banger.

The other 'slap' words are interesting. Slap-dash proclaims its meaning. But why does slap-up mean smart? And why should slapping and strapping both mean large and fine? A race run at a slapping pace suggests the whip. But 'a slapping gal' did not mean a miss likely to 'dot you one' but a handsome and attractive maiden, the counter-part of a fine, strapping fellow. He, in turn, was surely not so called because he was likely to 'give you strap', any more than the use of whopping for huge derived from flagellomania. But it does seem that the idea of potential violence was transferred to the semantics of size. A whopper by itself usually meant an enormous lie, which might, of course, involve a whopping. A slapping, slap-up fellow, seeking tick, might try to intimidate the owner of a slap-bang and be 'slapped down', if refused credit. Slap-happy, the recent usage, seems to mean either knocked silly or knocking carelessly about. It was an American's broadcast which labelled Goering as 'slap-happy Hermann'.

SLATE

S L A T E is 'an argillaceous rock of sedimentary origin', but, as a verb, it means not only to cover a roof with slivers of the said argillaceous rock but also 'to knock the hat over the eyes of a person'. This juvenile form of contumacious assault was extended and intensified to mean any kind of beating or drubbing. It is now most commonly used of critical and literary bastinado. 'He gave the book a good slating.' I cannot remember ever seeing it used of the old, hat-tilting insult. We have kept the slang usage of tile for hat, but I do not think slate is still employed in that sense.

Slatter, with the extra letter, is to spill or slop about. Hence the slattern which is a greasily descriptive word for an untidy or sluttish creature. Slut's origin is unknown. It is one of those expressive little words that seem to suggest themselves. The letters 'sl' have obviously seemed to the English the natural signals for dirty habits and things. We are slubbered with slob and slime, slush and sludge, until we become slubberdegullions; we are slip-slop slugs and sluts and slatterns. We slobber until we become slobber-chops. We live in slums in towns, among slag in mining-areas or in slumpy (boggy) places in the country. We slaver at the lips. In short, whenever we are filthily behaved or housed, we fall into the same alphabetical dishonour. And for punishment, the same letters come in powerfully, since we may be slapped, slammed and slogged as well as slated for our sins.

SLEAZY

IN one of those enchanting fourth 'leaders' in *The Times* I read 'In most of us the word hinterland suggests something stern and wild. It has the ring of a challenge. Beyond the sleazy, tropical port, beyond the semi-derelict railhead in the foothills of the plateau, out there, under the pitiless sun, stretches the hinterland, illimitable, imponderable, and inadequately mapped. It is — so at least we have instinctively supposed — a much tougher proposition than the interior'. I have surmised the author to be Peter Fleming. (I specialize in surmising the authorship of *The Times* fourth leaders by their vocabulary, quotations and general play of wit.) Mr. Fleming has made an extensive study of hinterlands in South America and elsewhere; he has also a very sure hand with words. But I was puzzled by sleazy. In the context I felt that it might be a telescopic form of slummy or sluttish and greasy. In that connection it seems to me an admirable adjective for a certain kind of tropical harbour.

But the dictionary tells me that it is thin and insubstantial; it is especially used of cloths and fabrics. So the leader-writer was visualizing a mere row of shacks and huts. But sleazy sounds wrong for thin; it oozes fatness of a nasty kind. A sleazy person is not, for me, a starveling, but one whose diet contains rich proportions of garlic and *fritto misto*, consumed with a cheap Chianti.

The leader on hinterlands pointed out that this word of menace has now become a tame piece of Planners' jargon. It is, for them, an 'urban sphere of influence'. Thus all our towns of any size, i.e. the unsleazy ones, have hinterland environs. 'The main difference in this respect between (say) Basingstoke and the Belgian Congo being that the Belgian Congo's hinterland is inside the Belgian Congo — whereas Basingstoke's hinterland is outside Basingstoke'. This is hard on the old romantic hinterlands of the novelists with their lone trails and sparse populations of despairing squatters and occasional decayed aristocrats who had been taken cheating at cards or passing 'dud' cheques and had retired to save the family's name from further degradation. I would expect to find sleazy (in my sense) types in a hinterland, but in planned Britain the hinterland mainly sprouts villas, garages and olde Tudor tea-shoppes.

SLEEP-WALKER

W H Y, I am asked, is there a word for sleep-walkers, but not for sleep-talkers? The former class is less common and frequently it mixes conversation with exercise, as in the case of Lady Macbeth. I see that the doctors have a Latin term for both, the somnambulants and the somniloquents. Commonest of all these releases for the subconscious distress or urge to communicate is talking to oneself while awake. Yet here again there is a blank. Self-talkers do not find a niche in the dictionary as such. Autophagous creatures eat themselves, a habit which the human race sometimes practises as far as the nails, though swallowing is here inadvisable. Autophobous folk are afraid of themselves. Autophonists might be speakers to themselves, since the Greek 'phone' is voice. But as a matter of fact they are much more complicated than that. Autophony is an attribute of self-doctoring and means 'observation of

the resonance of the speaker's own voice in auscultation'. Auscultation means listening with ear or stethoscope to the action of lungs,
heart, etc. I cannot find any recognition of autologists.

Matthew Arnold called Shakespeare 'Self-schooled, self-scanned,
self-honoured, self-secure', all of which adjectives, save perhaps
self-scanned, seem to me partly disputable. I fancy Shakespeare
must have been a self-talker: surely some of the magical lines
bubbled to his lips as he walked and pondered. He may too have
sleep-walked and sleep-talked, as there are many signs that he had
restless nights. It is the victim of insomnia who is most likely to
mutter aloud when he does drop off into a restless snooze.

It is plain to me that sleep-talkers have as much claim to acknowledgment by lexicographers as have the sleep-flower, which was
Francis Thompson's name for a poppy ('The sleep-flower sways in
the wheat') or the sleep-at-noon, which is the goat's beard that closes
its petals at midday.

SLOOMY

I N a book review in the *News Chronicle* Frederick Laws used the
adjective sloomy, claiming, justly, that it had the blessing of the
dictionary. It means sluggish, spiritless, dull and certainly would
suit some of the volumes which arrive on a book-reviewer's desk.
It has an agricultural and Scandinavian origin; it was used, 'of grain
not properly filled', and so, I suppose, empty of vitality. Above it
appears sloom, meaning a gentle sleep or slight doze, what the
Scots call a 'dwaum'. To those coping with a sloomy tome an
ensuing sloom is natural. A nice pair of dictionary neighbours.

Tennyson's *Northern Cobbler* spoke of 'sloomy Sally'.

SMOTHER

I A M always reading, in an England which has been for some years
almost vegetarian by compulsion, that what most people deeply
crave in the carnivore's way is 'steak smothered in onions'. We

think now of smothering as covering closely, but its original meaning came from dense smoke. When Orlando said 'Thus must I from the smoke into the smother', he meant going from bad to worse because smother (as a noun) was worse than mere smoke; it signified dense, stifling fumes. I do not suppose that a steak smothered in this sense would be popular, onions or no onions. Smother is one of the words which has declined in intensity; it was once a fearsome noun and verb, but now a tree can be agreeably smothered in its own foliage and a steak appetizingly smothered in onions.

Scotland has abundant words for smoke. Reek means only smell or stink in English ('reeking of alcohol' is not a kindly description of one who has had a social evening) but the reek of Auld Reekie is no worse than the fume of chimney-pots. Scotland has (or had) smeek, which is a happy mixture of smoke and reek. I came across that in a singularly cruel poem on Murray of Broughton, a man unpopular with Jacobites, to say the least of it. It begins 'Ken ye where cleekie Murray's gane?' That in itself is interesting because a cleekie was a stick crooked at the top and presumably gave its name to the golf-club, now almost forgotten, called a cleek. The dreary numbering of golf-clubs, which has banished cleeks, jiggers, mashies, niblicks and lofters in favour of Nos. 1 to 8 and even reduced the woods from drivers, brassies and spoons to bleak numbers also, is dreadful to me. How nice to think that, when you handled a cleek, you were also employing the synonym for dishonesty!

But I wander from smother and smeek. It was the same 'cleekie Murray' who evoked this query.

> Whare's his gowd and whare's his gain
> He rakit out 'neath Satan's wame?
> He has nae what'll pay his shot
> Nor caulk the keel of Charon's boat.
> Be there gowd where's he to beek
> He'll rake it out o' brunstane smeek.

I did not realize that to pay your shot was an eighteenth-century phrase. Beek is bathe or bask. Wame is womb or stomach. (Weem for cave, so common in Scottish place-names, is another form of it.) Gold 'rakit out 'neath Satan's wame', is superb for the traitor's fee. And brunstane smeek would be brimstone smother, not smoke, at least in old English, before smother had lost its horror and had become a verb for kindly covering the steak with the adorable — but not for the dyspeptics—fried onions.

SOSHERIE

S O S H is accepted English for a hard knock or a swashing blow. It rhymes appropriately with cosh. But a sosherie describes the vices of a deboshed company and does not make its way into O.E.D. I found it in that neglected story by John Galt *Ringhan Gilhaize* which I fancy some of the faithful Galtians and lovers of *Annals of the Parish* and *The Entail* have overlooked. The teller of the story tells of his grandfather, who 'came of a stock of bein burghers of Lithgow' and was saved from the Dominicans, 'those cormorants of idolatry'. So he regarded them, having come to Protestant austerity. The young Reformers were much abused by the followers of the old religion, but to no purpose. 'The persecutions which from that day the monks waged, in their conclaves of sloth and sosherie, against the children of the town, denouncing them to their parents as worms of the great serpent and heirs of perdition, only served to make their young spirits burn fiercer.' I like 'worms of the great serpent' almost as much as I like 'conclaves of sloth and sosherie'. Abominable as the cruelties of the Christian sects have been in their intemperate zeal for truth and for the putting down of error, they glorified our language with their rhetoric while they disgraced their faith by their dungeons and their faggots round the stake.

Jamieson's *Scottish Dictionary* gives the adjective Sosh, 'addicted to the company and the bottle', also 'snug, comfortable'. Presumably it is a popular corruption of social, a favourite adjective of Robert Burns for the comforting glass and companionable gaiety. But by linking sosherie with monkish sloth and crimes of oppression, Galt evidently thought badly of it. The English Latinism sodality for a company has no evil associations, despite the sound of it, and is associated much with ecclesiastical groupings. It is monkish, perhaps, but not a sosherie.

SPRUNKING

ROSE MACAULAY in her anthology 'The Minor Pleasures of Life' quotes *The Ladies Dictionary* (1694),

> This sprunking is a Dutch word, the first, as we hear, of that language that ever came in fashion with ladies.

The instances of the sprunking then employed indicate that it meant personal titivation. John Evelyn wrote

> Now therefore spare in the next place
> The pocket sprunking Looking-Glass;
> And that the cheeks may both agree
> Plumpers to fill the cavity.

There was much use of cosmetics and scents prescribed and then

> Thus rigged the Vessel, and equipped,
> She is for all Adventures shipped.

Montaigne recorded the bitter pains of sprunkery in Paris.

> I have seen some swallow gravel, ashes, coale, dust, tallow, candles and labour and toyle themselves to spoile their stomacke only to get a pale-bleake look.

A desperate flight indeed from rosy rapture. And in Barbary sprunking has meant self-mutilation of the horridest kind.

SPRUSH

I LEARN from Dr. Agnes Mure Mackenzie's *Scottish Pageant*
that 'the piece of joyous devilment called Johnnie Cope' was written
by a Lothian farmer, Adam Skirving, after the rout of the English
army under Cope by Prince Charlie's men at Prestonpans.

> Cock up your beaver and cock it fu' sprush,
> We'll ower the Border and gie them a brush,
> There's somebody there we'll teach better behaviour,
> Hey, brave Johnnie lad, cock up your beaver.
>
> Sawney was bred wi' a broker of wigs,
> But now he's gone southward to lather the Whigs
> And he's to set up as their shopman and shaver,
> Hey, brave Johnnie Cope, cock up your beaver.

Sprush is even better than spruce for jaunty neatness. It is full of
spit and polish. Trig, which may be a development of trick, is
another good Scots word for neat. If a man has been called
perjink, trig and sprush there is little more to be said of his nattiness.
When a beaver was slang for a beard and playing beaver was the
counting of beards encountered, the sprush beaver of Skirving's
song might have counted for two. In the late nineteen-forties
beards became too numerous to make the game worth playing
and most of them were not at all sprush.

Sawney, a variant on Sandy and so a name for any Scot, is
defined in English dictionaries as a term of derision: but here
Skirving used it proudly enough.

STEATOPYGOUS

STEATOPYGA, says my dictionary, is 'an accumulation of fat on the buttocks of certain races, e.g. Bushmen'. But why only 'certain races'? Is broadness of base to be thus restricted? The adjective 'steatopygous' is to be found in Aldous Huxley with reference to Aryans and also in Compton Mackenzie's riotously farcical novel of the old Highland gentry and their irritants, the Nationalists and the hikers. The reference, in *The Monarch of the Glen*, was not to kilted men but to trousered ladies, whose vogue of 'slacks' ill accords with any tendency to steatopyga.

Shakespeare had no such long names for broad beams. But he had closely considered the matter of rearward conformation; this is shown by the remarks of the Clown in *All's Well That Ends Well*. When the Countess of Rousillon said 'That's a bountiful answer that fits all questions', he replied, 'It's like a barber's chair that fits all buttocks — the pin-buttock, the quatch-buttock, the brawn-buttock, or any buttock'. Presumably brawn-buttock was Shakespearean for steatopyga: quatch applied to buttock is explained by the glossaries as squat or flat. But let us turn to loftier, if less fundamental, matters.

SURBATED

OVER-BEATEN, bruised, or made sore, especially used of overworked feet. Not having been brought up in Horseback Hall, I cannot be informative about the schedule in which it occurs, a colossal list of the diseases to which steeds are or were most liable. This was given in an Irish announcement of sale. It is common knowledge that speakers should be chary of using many words containing the letter 's' because they so easily make for hissing and spitting. This is particularly true of speech into the microphone. When addressing that implement I do my best to shun unnecessary sibilants. (Plenty of them in those last words!) Any broadcaster attempting to deliver the following advertisement would have an anxious time and, should he be one of those unfortunates who are endowed with excessive saliva, the 'mike' might need a towel afterwards. Here is the terrific statement, with its own grammar and spelling.

Sale at Skibbereen

Saturday, September 16th, 1769, will be sold or set up for sale, at Skibbereen, the robust horse Spanker, the property of Thomas O'Donnell, Esq., A strong, staunch, steady, sound, stout, sinewy, safe, serviceable, strapping, supple, swift, smart, sightly, sprightly, spirited, sturdy, sure-footed, shining, sleek, smooth, spunky, well-skinned, sized and shaped, sorrel steed of superlative symmetry, styled Spanker, and a snip, square-sided, slender-shouldered, smart-sighted, with a small star, and steps singularly stately; free from strain, sprain, spasms, string-halt, stranguary, sciatica, staggers, scalling, sollander, surfeit, seams, scouring, strangle, swelling, soreness, scratches, splint, squint, squirt, scruff, scales, scurvy, scars, scabs, scarred sores, scattering, shuffling, shambling gait or symptome of sikkness of any sort. He is neither stiff-mouthed, shabby-coated, sinew-shrunk, spur-galled nor saddle-backed, shell-toothed, slim-gutted, surbated, skin scabbed, short-winded, splay-footed or shoulder-slipped, and is sound in the sword point, and stiffle joint, has neither sick-spleen, sleeping-evil, set-fast or snaggle-tooth, nor suppression of urine, sand cracks, swelling-sheath, subcutaneous sores, or shattered hoofs, is not sour, sulky, slow, surly, stubborn, or sullen in temper, neither shy, sly nor skittish, sluggish nor stupid. He never slips, stripes, strays, stalks, starts, stops, shakes, swells, snivels, snibbles, snuffles, smarts, stumbles or stocks in his stall or stable; and scarcely or seldom sweats; has a showy, skittish, switch tail, or stern and a safe set of shoes to stride on. He can feed on stubbles, sheaf oats, straw, sedges, and scutch grass; carries sixteen stones on his stroke over a six-foot sod or stone-wall with surprising speed. His sire was the sly sober Sydus, a sister of Spindle Shank by Sampson and Sporter, son of Sparkler, who won the Sweepstake and Subscription Plate, last season at Sligo. His selling price is sixty-six pounds, sixteen shillings and sixpence sterling.

SUCCEDANEUM

HERE is a good thumping alternative for a substitute. It met the eye as I was making *Dombey and Son* the companion of a bed-ridden week. Captain Jack Bunsby of the *Cautious Clara* was encountered by Captain Cuttle and Florence Dombey wearing 'a dreadnought pilot-coat and a pair of dreadnought pilot-trousers whereof the waistband was so very broad and high that it became the succedaneum for a waistcoat, being ornamented near the bearer's breastbone with some massive wooden buttons like backgammon-men'. Another succedaneous article of this kind has been the Oriental Cummer-bund. In an age of drastic clothes-rationing, either by coupon or by height of price, the three-piece was commonly reduced to the two-piece suit in men's wardrobes; the waist-coat in Britain has been commonly succeeded by the pull-over or Cardigan, which has the merit of general service. But nobody now would portentously talk of his woolly as a waistcoat-succe-daneum.

There is an adjective succedaneous. It would be nice to see a masculine noun of this kind applied to relief-men in sports. In cricket-scores we read, when a succedaneous fielder has made a catch, 'Caught Sub. Bowled Googler'. Cricket scores have now to be abbreviated more than ever. To read 'Caught Succedaneous', would be a handsome change. But I suppose it would be cut to 'Ca. Succ., B. Googler' which is not so imposing to the eye.

Hard times bring wool-substitutes, meat-substitutes and faked alternatives of all kinds. Possibly a house-wife might be impressed by the announcement of an Egg Succedaneum; the contents would probably disappoint.

SWELTRY

T H A T good Georgian poet Lascelles Abercrombie in *The Sale of St. Thomas* used sweltry instead of sweltering and I think it is the better word, with its prickly blending of sweat and sultry.

> O horrible those sweltry places are,
> Where the sun comes so close, it makes the earth
> Burn in a frenzy of breeding — smoke and flame
> Of lives burning up from agoniz'd loam!
> Those monstrous sappy jungles of clutch'd growth,
> Enormous weed hugging enormous weed,
> What can such fearful increase have to do
> With prospering bounty? A rage works in the ground,
> Incurably, like frantic lechery,
> Pouring its passion out in crops and spawns.

This is the true terror begotten of extreme fertility in sweltry places. It makes one swelter to read it.

The old form of swelter was swelt, which meant to faint or make to faint, especially with heat. Shakespeare used sweltered oddly in *Macbeth*. The First Witch chants

> Round about the cauldron go,
> In the poison'd entrails throw,
> Toad that under cold stone
> Days and nights has thirty-one
> Swelter'd venom sleeping got,
> Boil thou first, i' the charmed pot.

This is usually taken to mean that the venom has been frigidly exuded, since the cold stone hardly suggests perspiration. Shakespeare drew on a book of 1591, *Newes from Scotland*, in which a woman accused of witchcraft 'confessed that she took a blacke toade and did hang the same up by the heeles, three days, and collected and gathered the venom as it dropped'. We might say now that a man in a Turkish bath is sweltering out some of his poisons in this sweltry spot.

TAPIST

THIS shortening of red-tapist, a bureaucrat, has dictionary acknowledgment. It is rare now and to most will suggest the refined stenographer instead of him who dictates to her the formidable lingo of the Whitehall ukase. But since this kind of taypist often works for Mr. Puffington and his kind, there is an added reason for not allowing the tapist label to be shed by Mr. Puffington himself.

TARGETEER

A FOOT-SOLDIER armed with a shield and a good-sounding fellow in romantic poetry. But now almost anybody. For the word, target, meaning not the shield that shielded but the shield that is shot at, and so the mark or goal, is on every politician's and economist's lips. 'The target is a million tons a day.' All workers and employers, if the word employer still means anything since the State so strictly controls them, imposing restrictions on the one hand and targets on the other, are our targeteers. But, whenever a word gets into Parliament and into the jargon of Ministerial Public Relations Officers, it is soon nonsensically dragged in. Here is Mr. Hector McNeil, Minister of State, saying

> it was distressing and bordering on dishonesty to make such a savage and substantial attack upon a Ministry and then to refuse to give the source of alleged information. *The information was 18 months after the target.* That kind of assertion was in line with the cheap, mischievous Tory propaganda that they met during the General Election.

So target has become all things to all men.

THROUGHLY

I T caused considerable indignation and even, I believe, punitive measures in a newspaper office when an announcement of the anthem 'Wash me throughly' appeared as 'Wash me thoroughly'. Yet the dictionary defines both as 'fully, completely'. The second form of the adverb does have a rather comic suggestion, as of vigorous scrubbing, which may be deemed unsuitable to the pious theme. The shorter word, throughly, has the dignity of an antique; the extra 'o' in the longer one carries the word from church to bath-tub. None the less, it seems to me to be foolish to make so much fuss about a printer's error, which, if you go by the lexicon, is not an error at all.

TOILET

H E R E is a curious progress of meanings. The toilette was originally a piece of cloth used for wrapping up clothes; it was also the towel or protective coverlet placed by the barber round the shoulders of his clients. From this it became the linen covering a dressing-table; then it was the table itself and all its appointments, the munitions of Venus. So Pope used it of Belinda,

And now, unveil'd, the Toilet stands display'd,
Each silver Vase in mystic order laid.
First, rob'd in white, the Nymph intent adores,
With head uncover'd, the Cosmetic pow'rs. . . .
From each she nicely culls with curious toil,
And decks the Goddess with the glitt'ring spoil.
This casket India's glowing gems unlocks,
And all Arabia breathes from yonder box.

The Tortoise here and Elephant unite,
Transform'd to combs, the speckled, and the white.
Here files of pins extend their shining rows,
Puffs, Powders, Patches, Bibles, Billet-doux.

It is interesting to learn that Belinda counted her holy writ in the plural.

So, in the age of the fops and belles, toilet came to mean not only the implements of beauty but the procedure of making-up. It could also signify a dressing-room reception of visitors or dress and decoration in general.

Finally America, in its search for exalted titles for the common 'convenience', a search which has given us the admirable Comfort Station, seized Belinda's toilet as one of its lavatory-labels. In this practice the polite sections of the European world have followed the Western lead. But when Pope wrote that 'the long labours of the toilet cease' he was not referring to ultimate victory over intestinal stasis. A small boy, with whom I was walking on Hampstead Heath, suddenly stopped and politely inquired, 'Is there a toilet here?'

TOOM

S O M E English dictionaries include toom for empty or desolate, although it is mainly used by Scots nowadays. Empty is a feeble little word for an idea which includes both the vastness of the desert and the bleak tragedy of want. Bare is much better. 'When she got there, the cupboard was bare' does call up the distress of those with naked larders. 'The cupboard was empty' would not be poignant at all. But 'the cupboard was toom' would utter the voice of real despair. Douglas Young, writing of the desolate Highlands, the great void of the far north, asks

What can ye shaw me here in this land of the Scots?
Breckans and maithie yowes and virrless stots,
Tuim untentit crofts where aathing rots.

This, in translation, is

> Bracken and maggoty ewes and emasculated bullocks,
> Empty, uncared for crofts where everything rots.

Tuim or toom sounds the mourning bell. And how much is gained by the broad double 'a' of aathing! 'Where everything rots' would be a commonplace statement of decay. But the 'aathing' comes rolling like a black cloud of misery over the untentit croft. It echoes most effectively the dead vast of barren solitude which is so curtly described by toom.

UMPER

IF you should find in an ancient text, with ancient spelling, the word umper you do but meet with an early version of the white-coated arbiter of ins and outs at a cricket-match. Lyly's Euphues was made an umper to decide in some contest. Does anybody know why the footballers refused to have umpers and preferred referees? The summer games, cricket and lawn-tennis, are faithful to the Norman umper while the winter sports of football and hockey are refereed. Racing men, neutral in this issue, abide by their Stewards' decision.

I called an umper a Norman because in French, and in a muddle, lies his origin. Professor Ullman in *Words and their Use* points out that

> Erroneous analysis may detach a sound from one word and add it on to another in its immediate vicinity. In English, the indefinite article has been particularly exposed to this treatment. An apron developed out of a napron, Old French naperon, 'napkin', an adder comes from a nadder, an auger from a nauger, an umpire from a numpire, Old French nomper 'peerless, odd man'. In all these cases, the initial n- of the next word was taken as belonging to the article. The reverse has occurred in a newt from an ewt and a nickname from an

ekename, where -n of the article has been added on to the next word. A similar shift is responsible for 'for the nonce', earlier for then once.

A nadder sounds certainly more venomous than an adder; the latter has a suggestion of blameless clerkdom. Indeed, to nadder might be a good verb for to sting. Theatrical producers and their actors can, if they wish to be precise, talk about a napron or a napkin stage. So the umpire is the exceptional man, the nonpareil. I have in the past done some service (of dubious competence) as an umper, and then I regarded myself as a drudge considerably put upon. It now appears that I was awarded loftier status. I was being unique.

VAUDEVILLE

VAUDEVILLE is now loosely applied to the music-hall and its products of all kinds. It was originally Chanson du Vau de Vire, a song of the valley of Vire in Calvados, Normandy. Calvados has produced a powerful liquor. This may have assisted Olivier Basselin who was said to be the father of Vaudevillian ballads. In the eighteenth century the name vaudeville was given to the song sung after a comedy. In this sense the Spring and Winter songs at the end of *Love's Labour's Lost* and Feste's *Hey ho the wind and the rain* are Shakespearean vaudevilles. Later on it was used of light shows and frisks of all kinds.

Although associated with merriment it is really too delicate a term for the rough buffooneries to which it has more recently been applied in our Palaces of Varieties. It suggests to me the wan Deburau who was the creator of Pierrot. It needs moonbeams for illumination, not a blaze of limelight. How many of those who have entered, in London or elsewhere, theatres named Vaudeville have thought of fifteenth-century Normandy and such a song out of a valley as our Christopher Fry might put into one of his medieval comedies?

VIRITOOT

W H A T is a viritoot? Something at least to which the gayer maidens of the Middle Ages brought the 'brisky juvenals' of the male sex. Consider this, from *The Miller's Tale*.

> This Absolon knokketh al esily,
> And seyde, 'Undo, Gerveys, and that anon.'
> 'What, who artow?' 'It am I, Absolon.'
> 'What, Absolon! For Cristes sweete tree,
> Why rise ye so rathe? ey benedicitee!
> What eyleth yow? Som gay gerl, God it woot,
> Hath brought yow thus upon the viritoot;
> By seinte Note, ye woot wel what I mene.

But do we ourselves wot well what this superb word indicates?

The glossary of the Globe Chaucer dodges it altogether. But it interprets Verytrot as quick-trot and implies that a Viritoot is a Very-trot. Other editions give viretote and then leave that unexplained. I like to think of viritoot as a Chaucerian spree or jaunt, made in the flush of spring and early manhood. In any case it is a gorgeous creation: let us recommend viritooting to the young and the 'gay girls' who can provoke it.

WHEECH

T H I S is a Scots word and must be pronounced with a soft 'ch' as in loch. The Wheech is not a Wheetch. I was given it in St. Andrews; perhaps the term lurks especially in the neuk of Fife. It means a twerp. Twerp has drifted out of English slang. We now more often call a feeble, foolish creature a drip, for which the Scots have dreep and dreepy. Wheech and Wheechy are still better. I can so easily visualize 'a wheechy wee mon'. But I insist that it must be wheechy in proper Scots and not wheetchy.

Wheech is also, I learn, used as a verb for 'to whip out or under'. A Scottish Home Guard sergeant invented a petrol-bomb to wheech under an oncoming tank. No wheech he!

WHISKIN

THE terminology of the tavern and its equipment has been rich in its time. One of the beautifully produced books on tavern-lore issued by the House of Whitbread — and at five shillings too! — quotes Heywood's *Philocothonistra or the Drunkard Opened, Dissected, and Anatomised* (1635).

> Of drinking cups, divers and sundry sorts we have, some of them elme, some of box, some of maple, some of holly, etc.; Mazers, broadmouthed Dishes, Noggins, Whiskins, Piggins, Crinzes, Ale-bowls, Wassal Bowls, Court dishes, Tankards, Kannes from a pottle to a pint, from a pint to a gill . . . Small jacks we have in many ale-houses of the Citie and suburbs, tip'd with silver, besides the great Black Jacks and Bombards . . . We have besides, cups made out of horns of beasts, of cocker-nuts, of goords, of the eggs of ostriches; others made of the shells of divers fishes. Come to plate, every taverne can afford your flat bowles, prounet cups, bear bowles, beakers. . . .

A whiskin had nothing to do with the usquebaugh or whisky which had reached London in Shakespeare's life-time. (The author of *The Great Frost; Cold Doings in London* (1607) mentions this blessing as one of the reliefs of an exceptionally hard winter.) The whiskin was a shallow vessel and Sir Walter Scott mentioned it as 'a black pot of sufficient double ale'.

The noggin was small, a pottle held two gallons. The mysterious crinze is defined as 'a stumpy, earthenware vessel which was a cross between a tankard and a small bowl'. The prounet or prunet was a liqueur-cup for drinking the strong distillation of wild plums, a tipple after the manner of sloe gin. Another vessel of the period was the Bellarmine, a sort of Toby Jug with a portrait of the hated Cardinal Bellarmine, oppressor of the Protestant potters. They had a small revenge by cartooning the grim ecclesiastic in their clay.

We meet the bombard in *The Tempest*. 'Another storm brewing', says Trinculo. 'I hear it sing i' the wind: yond same black cloud, yond huge one, looks like a foul bombard that would shed his liquor.' The Black Jack, a form of bombard, is visible, if I remember rightly, in Anne Hathaway's Cottage at Shottery near Stratford-upon-Avon. These are leather bottles.

The same book issued by Whitbread discusses the wine-labels of silver or enamel hung round the necks of decanters; also the old bottle-tickets.

Some curious and forgotten names appear on such as have come down to us. Who can say what is meant by 'Bounce', 'Nig', 'Mishianza', 'Bernis' or 'Hinojo'? Perhaps the silversmith found the writing of his original order difficult to read or perhaps the mistake originated in the order itself. A British traveller on the Continent might like the taste of a certain wine and order a quantity to be shipped home. He asks its name. Either he misunderstands the reply or by the time the wine arrives has only a hazy recollection of what was told him. A 'wine ticket' he must have, and so he writes down the name as near as he can remember it and gives it to the silversmith to copy. Yet even these explanations seem unsatisfactory when one is confronted with the extraordinary name of 'Zoobditty-match' on a label.

The Hinojo has a Spanish sound; so has Mishianza. Zoobditty suggests that some foreigner is trying to sing a song of soup. Bounce reminds me of James Bridie's cocktail discussed under the heading Lith.

WOMANIKIN

RICHARD CHURCH, who writes on 'Country Life' in *The Spectator* in English prose which is as good as his earthy and beflowered subject, makes this reply to a query about strange markings on the grass.

> Another reader is troubled about a fairy-ring on his lawn. I have one and accept it as a visitation from another, perhaps a lunar, world. I hope one night to go out and to encounter some panic womanikin, 'ill-met by moonlight,' dancing within that ring, or stroking Bottom's ears. But if our reader insists on being practical about this matter, he can probably dismiss his fairy-ring by watering it with a pound of sulphate of iron dissolved in three gallons of water.

It is pleasant to find the word panic used correctly and related to the god Pan and his magical, startling appearances. Womanikin may be called, I think, a piece of Church architecture. The dictionaries have never heard of it, but I find it a good mate to manikin. Presumably it is pronounced wománikin. The word womanikin surely need not be limited to the members of witch-covens and the like. It suggests all sorts of queer little parties to me, from the gay, wren-like Maria of *Twelfth Night* to the sharp rustic midgets who dart in and out of the stalls at country markets, with ruddy, wrinkled faces that remind one of apples in February.

ZEROISE

NOT a French two-syllabled adjective, but a three-syllabled verb, coming from the language of the Machine Age. 'When finished, please zeroise the dial'. That is certainly more brief than 'put the dial back to nought'. It would fit in with words like alerted. 'When alerted please unzeroise the dial'. Zeroise could also pass for one of those euphemistic substitutes for massacre so dear to the political cant of the dictatorships. Instead of saying that reactionary elements have been liquidated, the bulletin might announce that bourgeois objectivists have been zeroised. Objectivist is a recent addition to the lingo of Communist Orthodoxy. I presume that it means one who sees, or tries to see, realities plain and straight and is not to be upset by the subjectivism of propaganda. Thus objectivism ought to be the human ideal, but I gather from the neo-Marxist utterances that it marks the depth of human depravity and cries out for liquidation. If the verbose Marxians have not got on to zeroisation yet, they soon will.